HISTORY
IN CLOSE-UP

THE TWENTIETH CENTURY

COLOURPOINT
EDUCATIONAL

Sheila Turner Johnston

© Sheila Turner Johnston and Colourpoint Books
  2010

First Edition
First Impression

ISBN: 978 1 906578 44 2

Published by: Colourpoint Books
Layout and design: April Sky Design
Printed by: GPS Colour Graphics Ltd, Belfast

About The Author

Sheila Turner Johnston, BA, Dip Lib
Stds, had a career in both public and
educational librarianship before jointly
setting up Colourpoint Books in 1993.
She is now a writer and publisher.

She is the joint author of several
educational textbooks and author of
Alice: A life of Alice Milligan, published in
1994. She has won prizes for both fiction
and non-fiction and has published many
short stories. Her first novel, *Maker of
Footprints*, was published by Plover
Fiction in 2008.

COLOURPOINT
EDUCATIONAL

Colourpoint Books
Colourpoint House
Jubilee Business Park
Jubilee Road
Newtownards
County Down
Northern Ireland
BT23 4YH

Tel: 028 9182 6339
Fax: 028 9182 1900
E-mail: info@colourpoint.co.uk
Web site: www.colourpointeducational.com

TIP

PROJECT

BEFORE YOU START

ACTIVITY

BY THE WAY

SOURCES

WORD BOX

LINK

RESEARCH

A NOTE TO TEACHERS

When I set out to put together a text that would engage young people in the amazing twentieth century and address the requirements of the revised curriculum, I had ambitions to cover a hundred years in one sweep. That became manifestly impossible, unless the book were to become too big to get through the classroom door. I quickly realised how full to overflowing the twentieth century was with invention, achievement, tragedy and triumph.

Instead I have covered six topics in eight Units, which I hope will give ample scope for development in the classroom and will challenge and inspire pupils to use and expand on the skills needed to confront and engage in the world today, which is tomorrow's history.

So please do not blame me for omitting Topic X and Topic Y. I know there is so much more and perhaps many teachers may wish to use their own resources to cover events that I have not covered here. This is a book that will be best dipped into at any page, to fit in with your planned work scheme.

I am particularly indebted to Mrs Hazel Caldwell, Head of History at Regent House, Newtownards, who acted as a consultant on this project. Her wisdom, experience and – on occasion – frankness, have added so much to this text. Mrs Caldwell was unstinting in her help and encouragement and allowed me access to some of her own materials to keep me on the straight and narrow.

Because no Key Stage 3 textbook can leave out the compulsory Ireland topic, I have relied on some pages on the excellent book *Union to Partition*, by Dr Russell Rees and Miss Audrey Hodge, also published by Colourpoint and a classic textbook for many years. History teaching in Northern Ireland is indebted to both these authors for their many contributions right across the curriculum.

Last but not least, my husband Norman, an historian and a particular expert on transport history, was generous with his time and knowledge when I needed to pick his brain.

Any feedback, good or not so good, will be welcomed by both myself and the publisher. Such comments can only make better any subsequent printings.

Sheila Johnston
February 2010

INTRODUCTION

Read these quotations about history. Discuss each of them and decide what they mean.

> What is past is prologue.
> William Shakespeare, *The Tempest.*

> Until the lion has an historian of his own, the tale of the hunt will always glorify the hunter.
> African Proverb

> If you don't know history, you are a leaf that doesn't know it is part of a tree.
> Michael Crichton (paraphrased)

> If you would understand anything, observe its beginning and its development.
> Aristotle

> History is a vast early warning system.
> Norman Cousins

> History never looks like history when you are living through it.
> John W. Gardner

In 1900, Britain controlled nearly a quarter of the land in the world. The British Empire, through conquest and trade, had spread around the globe.

Today, the United Kingdom is made up of Great Britain and Northern Ireland. In 1900, it was the United Kingdom of Great Britain and Ireland.

Ireland was still ruled by Britain, although there had been several rebellions to try to gain independence. The representative of the Queen in Ireland was called the Viceroy or Lord Lieutenant. In 1900, the Viceroy was George Henry Cadogan, the Fifth Earl Cadogan. He was Viceroy from 1895 to 1902.

Queen Victoria was on the British throne, although she died in 1901. Victoria had been Queen since June 1837 and reigned for 63 years and 7 months, longer than any other British monarch. So people were very used to a long and stable 'Victorian era'. Many people had lived their whole lives with Victoria on the throne and couldn't remember any other monarch.

THEN ALONG CAME THE TWENTIETH CENTURY... THEN ALONG CAME THE T

It has been said that there was more change and development in the twentieth century than in all the centuries that had gone before. It was exciting, tragic, frightening, amazing, astonishing, horrible, wonderful, violent, depressing, enriching…

In fact, you've just got to discover some of it for yourself — read on!

GUIDE TO ICONS

 TIP

 PROJECT

 BEFORE YOU START

 ACTIVITY

 BY THE WAY

 SOURCES

 WORD BOX

 LINK

 RESEARCH

 QUESTION

SKILLS AND CAPABILITIES KEY

 COMMUNICATION

 MATHS

 USING ICT

 MANAGING INFORMATION

 THINKING, PROBLEM SOLVING, DECISION MAKING

 BEING CREATIVE

 WORKING WITH OTHERS

 SELF MANAGEMENT

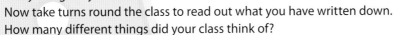

On your own, write down what you think money is needed for today. Think of as many things as you can.
Now take turns round the class to read out what you have written down.
How many different things did your class think of?

Now imagine you are living in 1900. Look at your list again. In 1900 do you still need money for all the things on your list?

Make a new list of all the things you could not buy in 1900.
What is money needed for in both 1900 and today?

Set out your results in a diagram like the one below. Copy this diagram into your notebook and fill it in.

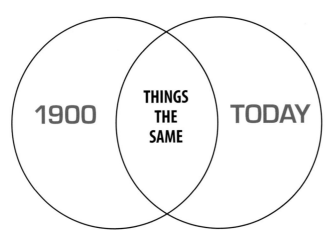

1900   THINGS THE SAME   TODAY

A lot of things happened to change the world between 1900 and 2000. Many of these events happened because of money or affected money in some way. Through looking at money we can also get a glimpse of some of the main events of the century.

Ordinary people like you and me need money, but countries and governments need money too.
A man called Mayer Amschel Rothschild said this in the eighteenth century:

> *Let me issue and control a nation's money and I care not who writes the laws.*

What do you think he meant?

Here are the events that we are going to look at in this Unit, and see how these events affected the money people used.

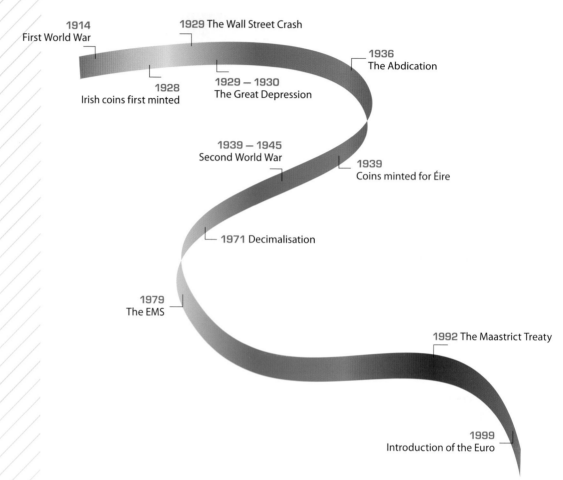

1914
First World War

1929 The Wall Street Crash

1936
The Abdication

1928
Irish coins first minted

1929 – 1930
The Great Depression

1939 – 1945
Second World War

1939
Coins minted for Éire

1971 Decimalisation

1979
The EMS

1992 The Maastrict Treaty

1999
Introduction of the Euro

Let's start by seeing what money looked like in 1900.

Have a good look at these two pennies. What is the same in both of them? What is different? What do you think is the biggest difference between them? Whose head is on each coin?

Here is a picture of a penny minted in 1901. This is its actual size.

This is a picture of a penny minted in 2000. It is shown at its actual size also.

Try this!

Gather several different coins. Cover one of them with thin white paper. It doesn't matter what side is up. Using a pencil with a fairly soft lead, scribble on the paper over the coins. Don't press too hard. You should see an impression of the coins appearing on the paper. You could do this with all your coins and then ask a partner if they can identify the impressions.

TIP

PROJECT

BEFORE YOU START

ACTIVITY

BY THE WAY

SOURCES

WORD BOX

LINK

RESEARCH

You have already read about Queen Victoria in the Introduction. Here are the sovereigns who have reigned after her in the twentieth century.

Edward VII
George V
Edward VIII
George VI
Elizabeth II

Activity

On your own or in pairs, find out when these sovereigns reigned.
Who was on the throne for the longest?
Who was on the throne for the shortest time?

MA

WO

....

All of these monarchs had images of their heads on the coins of the time – except one. We'll find out about that one later.

In 1900, there were not only pennies, but pounds also. They even had a £1 coin, although it didn't look like the one we have today. It was made of gold and was called a **sovereign**. There was also a **half sovereign**.

Sovereign   Half sovereign

SOVEREIGN: king or queen. Also a name for a coin worth £1.

MONARCH: another word for a king or queen.

CURRENCY: Something that is used to buy things. In our country and in most others, this is money.

Any maths to do with money was more complicated before 1971 than it is today. As well as the £1 and the penny, there was a third unit of currency – the **shilling**.

LINK TO FIRST WORLD WAR UNIT

In 1915, the sovereign and half sovereign were replaced by paper notes — the £1 note, and the ten shilling note. This was because of the enormous amount of money needed to pay for the First World War. Today's £1 coin was introduced in 1984 and the £1 note was withdrawn from circulation in 1988.

A one pound note

This is how the penny, shilling and pound worked:

There were 12 pennies in a shilling.

There were 20 shillings in a £1.

So how many pennies were in a £1?

If you had 24 pennies, this was 2 shillings.
This was written as 2/- or 2s 0d.

If you had 30 pennies, this was 2 shillings and 6 pence.
This was written as 2/6 or 2s 6d.

If you had 40 shillings, this was £2. This was written as £2-0s-0d.

We call pennies 'p' now. In old money pennies were called 'd'. So you would say, for example, "I'll give you **6d** for that pen." Now you might say, "I'll give you 30**p** for that pen."

Research

Find out what the 'd' stood for.

This photograph was taken inside the Belfast Co-operative Shop on the Ormeau Road in Belfast in 1935.

What do you see in this picture? How would you feel going into a shop like this today? How would you buy something in this shop?

This photograph was taken in 1907. It shows a snack bar in Carrick House, Lower Regent Street, Belfast.

Comment on this photograph. What do you notice about it?

About 1920, teas of bread, butter, jam, a slice of cake and a pot of tea could be bought for 1/6d (7.5p).

Research

In groups, plan a shop that you might have seen on the village street in 1910.

In your shop you will sell bread, milk, potatoes, tea, candles, a newspaper, biscuits and cheese.

Do some research to find out what price these items were in 1910.

Using a computer draw a plan of your shop showing were everything is. Make a price list for everything.

When you have finished, each group must explain how you researched your shop. What did you find most difficult? What did you find easiest?

Would you like to have lived when shops looked like this?

What would you like about them?

What would you not like about them?

When all the shops were small like this, how would life be different to today?

You could have a competition. Take it in turns for one person from each group to take a shopping list to another group and ask for the items they want. The person behind the counter must add up your bill in pounds, shillings and pence. **Remember!** – there were no calculators in 1910! But you can use a pencil and paper.

COM
MA
ICT
TPD
BC
WO

ERRAND: a journey to get, or do, something

RETAIN: keep

In groups

Divide into pairs

Half of the pairs must imagine they live in 1910 and describe the experience of a girl going to the shop with her mother. They live in a cottage about a mile from a village.
Describe their errand, right from the moment they set off. It is autumn and it might rain. What do they need to bring with them?
What is their journey like?
What do they see as they go?
What and how much are they likely to be buying?
On the wall of the shop is a picture of the monarch. Who is it?

The other half of the pairs are going to do exactly the same thing – but they are following the experience of a boy and his dad who live today. They live in the middle of a housing estate about half way along one of the main roads out of the town. They are going to shop in a supermarket.
Describe their errand, right from the moment they set off. It is autumn and it might rain.
What do they need to bring with them?
What is their journey like?
What do they see as they go?
What and how much are they likely to be buying?

When you have finished, join with another pair and discuss:

1. which lifestyle is preferable
2. what you would like to retain from the past

COM
MI
TPD
BC
WO

Spectrum debate

Imagine a line running all the way across your classroom. All those who think supermarkets are a really good idea should stand at one end. All those who think they are a really bad idea and who prefer smaller shops should stand at the other end. If you're not sure, stand in the middle.

Now someone who really likes supermarkets must try to persuade those who don't like them, or who are undecided, to come and join them. When one person is talking, no-one else is allowed to speak. Anyone who speaks when someone else is speaking must sit down and not take part any more!

Next, someone in favour of small shops must try to persuade the others to agree with him or her and join this group.

Anyone who moves up or down the line must explain why.

Which end of the line ends up with the most people?

Activity

Draw two spider diagrams. In the centre of one write 'Advantages of small shops' and in the centre of the other write 'Disadvantages of small shops'. Now fill in as much as you can. When you have finished, study them for a few minutes.

Which advantage do you think was the most important?

Explain to a partner why you think this.

Which disadvantage do you think is the most important?

Explain to a partner why you think this.

This is the Sainsbury's shop in Croydon about 1900.

This is the same shop in 1950 when it was converted to self-service.

By the middle of the century, **self-service shops** were beginning to appear. They started in the United States first and many shop owners here didn't think they would be popular. Sainsbury's opened their first self-service shop in Croydon in 1950. By 1962, about a quarter of all the food sold in Britain was sold by self-service shops.

What do you think is the difference between a self-service shop and a supermarket?

Source

Read this account of shopping before there were self-service shops.

"There were a lot of them. You never had to wait when you went in to a shop, unless you got an old farmer, or someone coming in to spend the morning talking to the shopkeeper. Or some of the women would come in and tell them all their troubles, but apart from that, there was no waiting. There was always plenty of people to serve."

Would you like to shop in a shop like this? Are there any things that would be good about it? What were the disadvantages?

Would you like to work in a small shop like this?

Extended writing

It is 1953. You have just been to visit the first self-service shop you have ever seen. You have to write an entry in your diary describing your experience. Write about how different it is to the shops you are used to. Describe how it looks and feels to you. Were some foods presented differently? How did you pay for your groceries? Where there many people there?

BY THE WAY In 1910, the Kirghiz people who lived in Central Asia still used horses as their main unit of money. Sheep were used for less expensive things and if you needed small change, you would have been given lambskins!

Irish coins

In 1928, the first modern Irish coins were minted.

Why do you think there had been no Irish coins and notes before this?

LINK TO
SECOND IRELAND
UNIT

Project

Your task is to discover what Irish coins were like after 1928.

You must: • find out what was the name of the country as it appeared on the coins. What did this mean?

• find out how many denominations of coins and notes there were.

• find out what design was the same on all the coins.

• find out what design was on the other side of each of the denominations.

• draw each of these designs on a large piece of paper.

• put your drawings up in a display. Label your display and each of the coins.

There was a change to Irish coins in 1939. The name of the country was different. Say why this happened.

The Republic of Ireland issued a ten shilling coin in 1966. It was a commemorative coin. What was special about the date 1966?

DENOMINATION: when used about coins, this refers to the units of coinage that were made. For example, 1p is a denomination; 50p is a denomination.

The Wall Street Crash and the Great Depression

PROSPERITY: great wealth

In 1929, there was a crisis in the banking system in the United States of America. The 1920s had been a great time of prosperity and many people had lots of money saved up in banks and invested in the Stock Market. But the banking system collapsed and the banks ran out of money. There were crowds outside each bank as people panicked and tried to withdraw their money. Many people who had been very rich lost all their wealth overnight. This event is regarded as the biggest financial crisis of the twentieth century, in the world.

A scene of panic on Wall Street.

The Wall Street Crash was one of the causes of a period of many years when people were much poorer and unemployment in the USA reached almost 13 million. These years are called the **Great Depression**. Families were made homeless and men who had once owned large companies had to look for work or even resorted to selling apples on the street. Some men even committed suicide. One family moved into a cave in Central Park in New York.

Sources

Read these accounts which were written during the Great Depression. Answer the questions which follow.

"Darwin's theory that man can adapt himself to almost any new environment is being illustrated, in this day of economic change, by thousands of New Yorkers who have discovered new ways to live and new ways to earn a living since their formerly placid lives were thrown into chaos by unemployment …

Two years ago citizens shied at jury duty. … But now things are different. The Hall of Jurors in the Criminal Courts Building is jammed and packed on court days. Absences of talesmen are infrequent. Why? Jurors get $4 for every day they serve.

…Now, in the Times Square and Grand Central zones, the sidewalks are lined with neophyte 'shine boys', drawn from almost all walks of life…

In one block, on West Forty-third Street, a recent count showed nineteen shoe-shiners. They ranged in age from a 16-year-old, who should have been in school, to a man of more than 70, who said he had been employed in a fruit store until six months ago…

Shining shoes, said one, is more profitable than selling apples – and he's tried them both.

'You see, when you get a shine kit it's a permanent investment,' he said, 'and it doesn't cost as much as a box of apples anyway.'

According to the Police Department, there are approximately 7,000 of these 'shine

TPD

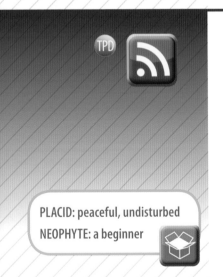

PLACID: peaceful, undisturbed
NEOPHYTE: a beginner

boys' making a living on New York streets at present. Three years ago they were so rare as to be almost non-existent, and were almost entirely boys under 17. Unemployment has brought back the newsboy in increasing numbers. He avoids the busy corners, where news stands are frequent, and hawks his papers in the side streets with surprising success. His best client is the man who is 'too tired to walk down to the corner for a paper.' "

New York Times, 5 June, 1932

"There is not a garbage-dump in Chicago which is not diligently haunted by the hungry. Last summer in the hot weather when the smell was sickening and the flies were thick, there were a hundred people a day coming to one of the dumps. A widow who used to do housework and laundry, but now had no work at all, fed herself and her fourteen year old son on garbage. Before she picked up the meat, she would always take off her glasses so that she couldn't see the maggots."

Edmund Wilson, *New Republic*, February, 1933

> DILIGENTLY: with great care
> GARBAGE: rubbish

1. Are these primary or secondary sources?
2. In the first source, one man comments that getting a shine kit is a permanent investment. What does he mean by this?
3. Do either of these writers seem to be sympathetic to the plight of the unemployed?

Activity

You and a film crew have been sent onto the streets of New York to film a five minute report for the evening news, on the circumstances of the unemployed. Write a script for your report which will be given live to camera as you walk.

> ### Can you find the answers to these questions?
> Where is Wall Street?
> Who was the President of the United States at the time?
> Who was the Prime Minister in the United Kingdom in 1929?
> In which state in the USA is the City of Chicago?

Project
Write a biography

Money is often the reason why some people turn to crime. There was a notorious gangster who lived in Chicago in the 1920s. His name was Al Capone.

Divide into groups and give your group a name. Think of something really catchy! Each group must put together a biography of Al Capone.

In your groups, talk about how you will go about

> NOTORIOUS: well known for bad reasons

writing your biography. Everyone in the group must contribute something. A biography must cover the whole of a person's life, so you should include sections on:

- when and where he was born.
- who his parents were and what they did for a living.
- where he was brought up.
- what he was like as a person. Include a picture if you can.
- what he did during his life.
- when and where he died.
- what caused his death and where he is buried.

When you have gathered all your facts, write out a first draft of your biography. Everyone in the group must read it and make comments. Maybe someone might think of a better way to say something, or maybe one person might realise that an important fact has been left out. Everyone must listen to the points others are making. If there are different opinions on something, then you must talk it over and decide on a way forward that every one can agree on.

Word process your biography neatly. Give it a title page and type in the name of your group as the 'Author'.

Include a contents page.

Put together an index at the back.

When all the groups have finished, one person from each group must talk about their biography and how they went about writing it.

What did you find most interesting about Al Capone?

If you could meet him, what questions would you like to ask him?

What words would you use to describe him? Write down a list of these words.

. . . .

Review your work

Do you think your group worked well together?

Were you pleased with your finished biography?

What are the advantages of writing a first draft?

What two things did you do really well?

What do you think you could have done better?

Now complete this sentence: "By doing this task, I have learned …"

TIP

PROJECT

BEFORE YOU START

ACTIVITY

BY THE WAY

SOURCES

WORD BOX

LINK

RESEARCH

The Abdication Crisis

Edward and Mrs Simpson

You have seen that an image of the reigning monarch appears on all coins in the UK. There was one king whose image does not appear on any coin.
He was **Edward VIII**.

When George V died in 1936, his eldest son became Edward VIII. However, Edward fell in love with an American woman, **Wallis Simpson**. She was a divorcee. At that time this was much more unusual than it is today and there was a stigma attached to it. Parliament, the royal family and many of the people of Britain were strongly of the opinion that they did not want a divorced American woman to be the Queen.

Stanley Baldwin was the Prime Minister at the time and he told Edward that he could either marry Mrs Simpson or he could be King – he could not do both.

Edward decided that he could not give up Mrs Simpson and so he abdicated the throne and his younger brother became George VI. Edward married Wallis Simpson and they lived most of the rest of their lives in Paris.

So Edward became king in January 1936 and abdicated in December 1936. He was never officially crowned at a coronation ceremony and is sometimes known as 'the uncrowned king'. He was king for less than a year and no coins were minted with his head on it.

The Abdication of Edward VIII was a really big event. This was the first time in history that a monarch had given up the British crown voluntarily.

ABDICATE: to give up
STIGMA: a mark of disgrace
VOLUNTARILY: of your own free will

In pairs, produce a report on the abdication of Edward VIII. In your report you should include answers to these questions:

- Why and when did Edward become king?
- What was he like as a person?
- Why could he not marry Wallis Simpson and remain as king? You may find several reasons for this.
- What did the royal family think at the time?
- Who became king after him?
- Was the next king glad to take over? Explain your answer.
- Who was the new king's wife?
- Who is the new king's daughter?
- What major world event happened three years after the Abdication?

Plan how you will go about your research. Divide up the task between the two of you. Try to find illustrations to include. Perhaps you could even draw some illustrations yourself.

Word process your report neatly. Include a cover page and an index.

ICT

MI

TPD

BC

WO

SM

LINK TO FIRST WORLD WAR UNIT

Money and War

There were two World Wars in the twentieth century.

The First World War started in 1914 and lasted until 1918.

The Second World War started in 1939 and ended in 1945.

Q Who was on the throne in the UK when the First World War started?

Q Who was on the throne in the UK when the Second World War started?

A country needs a lot of money in order to go to war.

Q Can you think of reasons why war is expensive? What does a government need to purchase at times of war?

When so much money is needed for fighting, there is less money around for food and clothing. During the Second World War, many things were rationed. Each family was given coupons for things like eggs and butter. Meat was specially scarce.

Members of the Women's Land Army harvesting beet, about 1942

Another way to obtain food was to grow it yourself. Many young women joined the Land Girls. These were girls who went to live on farms and helped in the fields with sowing and harvesting.

Q What other things could women do during the war?

Q Why do you think many women took on agricultural work during the wars?

The Big Change! 15 February 1971

During the twentieth century one of the biggest changes to our money took place. Instead of pounds, shillings and pence, we changed over to having just pounds and pence. Money maths got a lot easier too because now there were 100 pennies in £1 – and that was it! This change in our money was called **decimalisation**. People shortened this to 'D Day'.

 The phrase 'D day' was used before in the twentieth century. Can you find out when and why?

Because there were now only 100 pennies in a pound instead of 240, each new penny was worth more than an old penny. When shopping, it helped to remember that 5p was equal to the old shilling. 50p was half of a pound. What was half of a pound in 'old money'?

> Q Find out what the prefix 'deci-' means.
> How many other words can you think of that begin with 'deci-' or 'deca-'?

We see our decimal coins every day, but here is one you may not have seen.

Actual size.

This little coin was withdrawn from circulation in 1984. Can you think of reasons why it was withdrawn?

It was hard to get used to the 'new money' at first. Read these accounts from three people who remember the change-over and answer the questions that follow.

"My parents ran a small business in 1971 selling and repairing cash registers which were mainly sold to small corner shops and the like in the North Midlands.
For us D [Decimal] Day was a great money spinner converting or selling new or dual machines.
I was 15 and remember the heartache and problems that D Day caused however. Not only did prices rise and the general public had problems with the change-over, but the level of effort involved for small businesses to cope and manage was tremendous.
There was little help provided and a number of small corner shops went out of business simply because of this change."

"I was 14 in 1971 when we switched away from pounds, shillings and pence and my main memory is of the TV advertising campaign that tried to convince us that the switch would be so easy.

I have never seen anything since that has made such a dog's breakfast of a really simple concept – no wonder most folk wandered round in a state of total confusion. If you recall most people couldn't get a grip on the fact that both 4d and 5d were worth 2p in the new cash – significant when a Kit Kat was 4d and a Mars Bar 5d."

"I remember my latter years at Primary School (late sixties, beginning of seventies) having lessons in the 'new' money. We all thought the same: 'How on earth will we ever be able to calculate prices of anything?' At the time the thought of trying to convert Shillings into 'New Pennies' was horrifying. Looking back I can't believe we put up with the old currency for as long as we did. The other thing I distinctly remember was how everything became more expensive under the new system!"

Source: news.bbc.co.uk/onthisday/hi/witness/february/15/

1. What words would you use to describe how each of them felt at the time?
2. From reading these accounts, who and what were the things that were affected by the change-over?
3. Can you think of any other ways in which life was affected?
4. Who was the change-over most difficult for? Explain why you think this.
5. Who would have found the change-over very easy? Why do you think so?

Activity

Do you know anyone who remembers decimalisation? If they are willing, interview them about it. Ask how they felt and what decimalisation meant to them. Report back to the class.

The Irish Republic

The Irish Republic has had two big changes in its currency. The Republic changed over to decimal currency on the same day as the United Kingdom. Then, in 2002, its government changed over to the new European common currency, the Euro (€).

> LATTER: the last
>
> IMPORTS: goods brought into a country from another country

The Euro

Since the end of the Second World War in 1945, many politicians had been considering ways to bring European countries together to try to ensure that a war was much less likely to happen again. In 1957 the Treaty of Rome was signed by six countries: West Germany, France, Italy, Belgium, Netherlands and Luxembourg. These six countries agreed to trade freely with each other without customs. They also agreed to charge about the same rate of tax on imports into each of their countries. This group of countries was called **The European Economic Community (EEC)**. Sometimes it was referred to as The Common Market.

The **European Community** (EC) was set up in 1967. The UK Prime Minister at that time was a Conservative, Edward Heath and he was very much in favour of the UK becoming more closely involved with Europe. In 1973, the United Kingdom joined it, along with Denmark and Ireland. However, it was a very controversial decision and the Conservative party lost the next General Election.

The new Prime Minister, Harold Wilson, was from the Labour Party. In 1975, he held a referendum on whether people wanted to stay in the EC. Everyone who normally voted in elections was able to vote in this referendum. 66% of voters voted to stay in the EC.

According to the Treaty that set up the EC, it was meant to establish "an area without frontiers in which the free movement of goods, persons, services and capital is ensured." It was also to "preserve peace and liberty and to lay the foundations of an ever closer union among the peoples of Europe."

> CONTROVERSIAL: open to much debate
>
> REFERENDUM: a vote taken to find out the views of voters on a particular issue

In 1991, political leaders from the EC met at Maastricht in The Netherlands. John Major was the Prime Minister of the UK.

The **Maastricht Treaty** set up the **European Union** in 1993. This treaty drew its members closer together politically as well as economically. The countries that signed it agreed to go over to a common currency, to be used by all of them. John Major, however, negotiated an 'opt-out' clause for the UK. This meant that the UK was part of the EU but did not have to be part of the single currency. So the UK kept the pound. In 2002, there were 15 member countries in the European Union. On 1 January, twelve of them started to use the Euro as their everyday money. This change was even bigger than the change to decimalisation in the United Kingdom. In these twelve countries, more than 6 billion notes and 40 billion coins were distributed. Banks, shops and cash machines all had to be stocked with the new money.

BY THE WAY

When the Euro was introduced, the former coins and notes weren't used any more. Some people collect old coins. The hobby of collecting coins is called numismatics. Numismatists may collect coins from Roman times or even earlier.

Three countries in the EU refused to change to the Euro. They were the United Kingdom, Sweden and Denmark.

Find out what currencies each of these three countries use.

The Euro is a decimal currency. This means that there are 100 cents in one Euro.

Euro coins all have the same design on one side but each country can put its own design on the other side.

Wherever you go in the 'Eurozone' (countries that use the Euro) you can use the same money, no matter which country it came from originally.

These are the members of the European Union today.

1. Austria	11. Greece	21. Portugal
2. Belgium	12. Hungary	22. Romania
3. Bulgaria	13. Ireland	23. Slovakia
4. Cyprus	14. Italy	24. Slovenia
5. Czech Republic	15. Latvia	25. Spain
6. Denmark	16. Lithuania	26. Sweden
7. Estonia	17. Luxembourg	27. United Kingdom
8. Finland	18. Malta	of Great Britain and
9. France	19. Netherlands	Northern Ireland
10. Germany	20. Poland	

Read these and try to memorise them!

TIP

A good way to remember a long list is to memorise it in bits. Memorise the first four. Then close your book and try to write these four down. Then memorise the next four and so on. There are 27 in all. 27 doesn't divide evenly by four. How many countries will be in the last batch you have to remember?

With a partner, take a page each and draw a line down the middle. Label one column 'Advantages of a single currency' and the other column 'Disadvantages of a single currency'. Write down as many advantages and disadvantages as you can think of, then swap pages with your partner.

How many things do you and your partner agree on? Do you disagree on anything? If so, discuss why you disagree.

Now discuss in class all the factors you have thought of.

TIP

PROJECT

BEFORE YOU
START

ACTIVITY

BY THE WAY

SOURCES

WORD BOX

LINK

RESEARCH

The European Economic Community, set up by the Treaty of Rome in 1957

West Germany
France
Italy
Belgium
Netherlands
Luxembourg

European Union in 1993, set up by The Maastricht Treaty

Austria
Belgium
Denmark
Finland
France
Germany
Greece
Ireland
Italy

Luxembourg
Netherlands
Portugal
Spain
Sweden
United Kingdom of
Great Britain and
Northern Ireland

Members of The European Community in 2009

Austria
Belgium
Bulgaria
Cyprus
Czech Republic
Denmark
Estonia
Finland
France
Germany

Greece
Hungary
Ireland
Italy
Latvia
Lithuania
Luxembourg
Malta
Netherlands
Poland

Portugal
Romania
Slovakia
Slovenia
Spain
Sweden
United Kingdom
of Great Britain
and Northern
Ireland

Automatic Teller Machines

Banks used to have short opening hours so that it was difficult for people to get to them, specially when they were working all day. As the twentieth century went on, banks became so busy when they were open that the queues got longer and longer.

You will have seen machines like the one in the picture, often set into a wall near shops and banks.

These are Automatic Teller Machines, or ATMs for short. Most people who have a bank account are given a card which they can insert into this machine. They type in a password and can withdraw money from their account without having to go into the bank or queue at the counter.

In 1967, the first ATM was installed by Barclay's Bank in Enfield, Middlesex. Early ATMs didn't use a card. Bank customers were given a token to insert into the machine.

Credit cards

Credit cards are used almost everywhere instead of cash today. But did you know that there were no credit cards in the UK until the 1960s? The very first card that could be called a credit card was the Diners' Club card. This was issued in the United States and could be used only in some restaurants in New York.

In 1967, Barclay's Bank issued the Barclaycard. This was the first credit card which was used much like we use one today.

(COM)
(TPD)
(BC)
(SM)

Class Debate

Organise a class debate on the motion "This house believes that credit cards should never have been invented."

Before the debate starts, each person should write down on a piece of paper whether they agree with the motion or not.

Appoint a Chairperson and two main speakers: one to support the motion and one to oppose it. After they have spoken, anyone in the class may speak, but only for two minutes. Perhaps there could be a 'timer' who could ring a bell or tap the desk when the speaker's time is up.

After the debate, how many people have changed their minds?

Those who have changed their opinion should explain to the class what arguments influenced them.

Class Quiz!

Divide into two teams and decide on a prize for the winning team. If you get a question right, your team gets a point, BUT if you get a question wrong, you lose a point!

1. After 1928, Irish coins had a harp on one side. What was on the other side of an Irish 2/- piece?
2. There has never been a ten shilling coin. True or false?
3. Why were there no coins with Edward VIII's head on them?
4. Who was the monarch who came after George VI?
5. What year was the modern £1 coin introduced?
6. What was the date of the Maastricht Treaty?
7. Where did Sainsbury's open their first self-service shop? When?
8. When was the Treaty of Rome signed?
9. What countries signed it?
10. How many members are there in the European Union today?
11. What three countries in the EU still don't use the Euro?
12. Who was the Prime Minister during the Abdication Crisis?
13. When did Edward VIII abdicate? Give the month and year.
14. In which of the United States is the City of Chicago?
15. What is a biography?
16. What do the letters 'ATM' stand for?
17. How many old pennies were in a pound?
18. In what year did the Wall Street Crash happen?
19. When was decimal coinage introduced in the UK?
20. What is the name for people who collect coins?

Your Timeline

Draw a timeline and mark on it all the dates that you have read about in this chapter and what happened on those dates.

Word Check

Check out these words to make sure you can spell them.

government	circulation	biography
sovereign	Luxembourg	referendum
monarch	Netherlands	numismatics
calculator	European	password
advantage	abdication	currency
commemorative	Churchill	coupon
decimalisation	automatic	

If you're not sure if you can spell any of them, check them out a few more times.

BEFORE YOU START

In 1900, Ellen Key wrote an international bestseller called *The Century of the Child*. She thought that the welfare of children was the most urgent matter that society had to deal with in the twentieth century. Read the following extract from her book:

> "Filled with sad memories or eager hopes, people waited for the turn of the century, and as the clock struck twelve, felt innumerable undefined forebodings…
>
> The events at the turn of the century caused the new century to be represented as a small naked child, descending upon the earth, but drawing himself back in terror at the sight of a world bristling with weapons, a world in which for the opening century there was not an inch of free ground to set one's foot upon."

The Century of the Child, Ellen Key, published 1900

1. What kind of a world does Ellen Key think exists at the beginning of the twentieth century?

2. Does Ellen Key think that the new century will be good for children? Explain your answer.

3. What does "innumerable undefined forebodings" mean?

During the twentieth century, the standard of living for families in Britain and Ireland improved greatly. At the beginning of the century, there was a great difference between the lives of the rich and the poor.

In 1900, the health of children was not nearly as good as it is now. This was mostly because of **poverty**.

The life expectancy of babies born, 1901–1999		
1901	boys	45 years
	girls	49 years
1911	boys	50 years
	girls	55 years
1930	boys	59 years
	girls	63 years
1950	boys	64 years
	girls	67 years
1970	boys	69 years
	girls	73 years
1999	boys	75 years
	girls	80 years

Sources: Central Statistics Office and Office of Health Economics

Activity

Present the statistics in the table above as a graph.

What do you notice about these statistics?

Do you think the statistics are easier to analyse in a table or in a graph?

Poverty in the early 1900s was widespread among working class people. This was really serious poverty. It wasn't like not being able to afford to buy the latest DVD; many families went hungry because they couldn't buy food.

Four basic human needs:

Food

Heat

Shelter

Clothing

TPD

SM

Activity

List what you think are necessary items to own nowadays.

Now imagine that you have to give up all these things one at a time. Arrange them in order of importance to you.

Which one would you find easiest to give up? Write about 60 words explaining why.

Which one would you find hardest to give up? Write about 60 words explaining why.

Compare your choices with the rest of the class.

When you have heard about other people's choices, do you feel like changing your mind on any of your own? If so, why?

At the start of the twentieth century, 15% of families were living at subsistence level. That means that they could just about afford basic human needs but nothing else at all. Moreover, 10% of families were living *below* subsistence level. This meant that they couldn't even afford such basic things as a healthy diet.` Mothers made clothes from rice or flour bags which they got from the grocer's. Babies were put down to sleep in an open drawer or perhaps in an orange box from the greengrocer. By the age of 10, there might be as much as five inches difference in height between a boy from a poor family and a boy from a wealthy family.

Even if you could afford some food, it might not be good food such as fresh fruit and vegetables. Without these, you don't get enough vitamins, minerals and protein to be fully healthy. Here are some of the consequences of malnutrition:

- diseases like rickets (a childhood disorder involving softening and weakening of the bones, because of lack of Vitamin D and calcium)
- depression
- gum disease and poor teeth
- pregnant women have underweight and weak babies
- lower intelligence
- lethargy

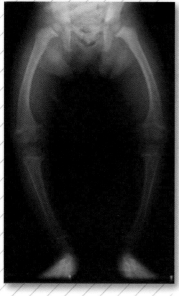

An X-ray of the legs of a two-year-old with rickets.

Activity

Ada Ballin was a writer and feminist who died in 1906. Here is an extract from a book she wrote:

> In England more than half of all the children die under twelve years of age, and they die chiefly from insufficient clothing… From one point of view only can anything be said in its favour, and that is, allowing there are already too many people in the world, it will be an advantage to get rid of as many of the weakest of the newcomers as possible.

The Science of Dress, London: Sampson Low, 1885

LETHARGY: a feeling of being tired.

MALNUTRITION: the result of an unbalanced diet.

TIP

PROJECT

BEFORE YOU START

ACTIVITY

BY THE WAY

SOURCES

WORD BOX

LINK

RESEARCH

What do you think of Ada Ballin's views in this extract?

Do you think she is in favour of letting weak babies and children die?

Pick out words from the following list which you feel best describe the tone of this extract:

**sympathetic   cold   kind   cruel   judgemental
loving   arrogant   logical**

In 1901, a man called **Seebohm Rowntree** wrote a report on the poor people of the city of York in the north of England. He was from a Quaker family which owned a chocolate factory in the city.

BY THE WAY

Rowntree's was started way back in 1725 by Mary Tuke. She came from a prominent Quaker family. When she was 30, she set up a grocery shop in York. This was an unusual thing for a woman to do at this time.

Seebohm Rowntree said in his report that a quarter of all families "… must never spend a penny on a railway fare or an omnibus… they must never purchase a half-penny newspaper… the children must not have pocket money or dolls or sweets or marbles… the wage earner must not be absent from his work for a single day."

Class discussion

1. Discuss the consequences of not being able to travel, or to buy a newspaper. What effect would this have on you?

2. Think of a major news event that you remember. How did you find out about it? Imagine you lived without television, radio, the Internet, books or newspapers. How would you find out what was going on? How would you know if the information you heard was accurate?

3. Some day in the future, the years you are living through now will be history! How will historians in the future find out about people, things and events today?

In 1906, there was a General Election and a Liberal government was formed. They introduced free school meals for poor children, so this was of some help in making children healthier.

Many years later, in 1944, the Education Act required all local authorities to provide meals and free milk to school children every day. Pupils also got a health check-up.

As you can see, many of the things we take for granted today were not always available. Charities also helped out poor families. For example, there were Boot Funds set up which provided footwear for the children of those families who couldn't afford it.

Research

There are some major charities still around today that have been helping poor and neglected children for over a hundred years. One of these is Barnardo's. When Thomas Barnardo saw how extreme poverty was causing suffering to so many children in London, he set up a Ragged School in 1867. Thomas Barnardo died in 1905.

In groups, investigate the history of Barnardo's.

Choose what to do with your findings. You could do one or more of the following:

- Outline the work of the charity from its founding to the present day, showing how the work has changed over the years. How different is it now compared to its early years? Why do you think its work has changed?

- Create a story board of Dr Barnardo finding some children sleeping on the streets and taking them to safe shelter.

- Create a five minute presentation to give to the class. Include PowerPoint slides.

- Design an information leaflet on the work of Barnardo's. Include a request for donations.

- Imagine you are a homeless child in London in 1902. Tell a friend about what happened when someone from Dr Barnardo's found you and took you to a safe place. Use your imagination! What family have you come from? How did you end up on the street? What are you feeling and thinking, before and after you are rescued?

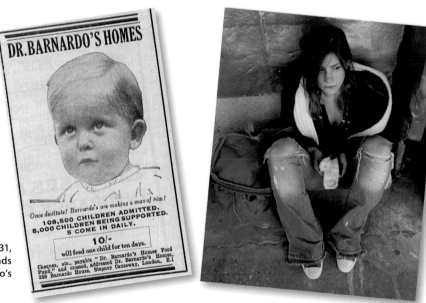

A poster from 1931, appealing for funds for Dr Barnardo's

Review

Where did you find most of your information for this research? Were you happy with your sources?

Would you like to know anything else about Barnardo's, or about life for children in the early 1900s?

If you could talk to Dr Barnardo, what would you say to him? What questions would you ask him?

As the century went on, conditions eased a little because governments introduced more benefits that could be paid to families. For example, the **Family Allowance** was introduced in 1946. This gave a payment to families for each child except the first one. After the Second World War, parents were encouraged to bring up more children because so many people had died. The **National Health Service**, introduced in 1948, brought a very significant improvement in people's health. Then, in 1975, a payment was given to families for all children, including the firstborn.

LINK TO MEDICINE UNIT

If you were born into a wealthy family, your life was very different. You might have had a nanny like the one in the photograph on the right to look after you and you would have had plenty of food and clothing. During the Edwardian years (the years when Edward VII was king, 1901–1910), babies and young children received more attention that they had before. More books were written on baby and child care and dedicated products, such as prams, nursery furniture and special clothes for babies, were developed further.

At first, prams were very expensive and not very safe. There were no brakes and the wheels didn't swivel to turn corners. There were no straps to hold the baby or toddler in. By the 1920s, prams were cheaper and a bit safer. They had larger wheels and deeper bodies to stop the baby falling out.
From the 1970s, adaptable pushchairs became more common and heavy prams are seldom used today.

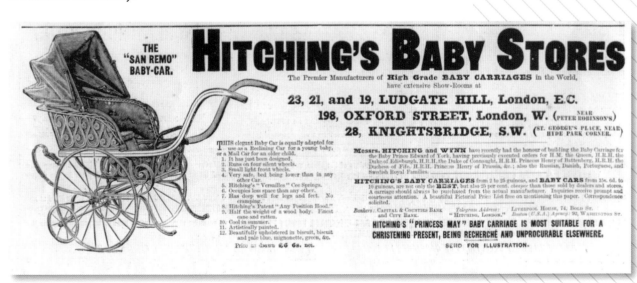

An advertisement from *The Illustrated London News* of 1895.

Activity

Why do you think pushchairs are more popular now? What has changed since the beginning of the twentieth century to make lighter, more adaptable pushchairs more popular than prams?

BY THE WAY

The word 'pram' is short for 'perambulator'.

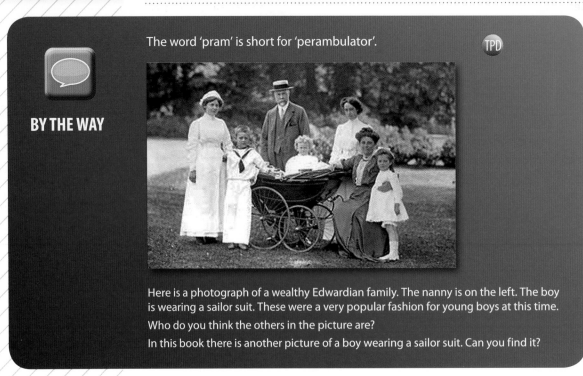

Here is a photograph of a wealthy Edwardian family. The nanny is on the left. The boy is wearing a sailor suit. These were a very popular fashion for young boys at this time.
Who do you think the others in the picture are?
In this book there is another picture of a boy wearing a sailor suit. Can you find it?

In very wealthy families the children lived in the nursery with the nanny. They ate their meals there too. Children might be brought down to see their parents only once a day. It was an important occasion in a child's life when he or she was allowed to dine with the adults for the first time.

Increasingly, in middle-income families, the whole family ate meals together. Meals were more formal than they often are today. They were at a set time and the members of the family talked to each other and discussed the events of the day. Children had to behave well and could be banished from the table if they showed bad manners.

In groups, discuss the following questions:

- From the child's point of view, are there advantages to eating separately from adults?
- Why might wealthy parents want to see their young children only once a day?
- What are the advantages of all eating together as a family?
- Discuss the various ways in which we eat our meals now. Describe how you think meals should be taken. Who would be there? Where would you eat? Who would cook the food? Who would clear up afterwards? Would you talk to each other or watch television?

TIP

PROJECT

BEFORE YOU START

ACTIVITY

BY THE WAY

SOURCES

WORD BOX

LINK

RESEARCH

Project

Write a biography

Dr Benjamin Spock was a paediatrician (pronounced *pee-dee-a-trishon*: a doctor for babies and children) who lived through nearly the whole of the twentieth century.
In 1946, he published a book called *The Common Sense Book of Baby and Child Care.*

Research the life of Dr Benjamin Spock and write a short biography of him. Include details on why his book was important and how his advice was different to childcare practice that had gone before.
As the final section of your biography, give your own opinion on the advice of Dr Spock and whether or not you think he was right.

COMPULSORY: required; has to be done.

ENFORCE: to make happen.

Education

Towards the end of the 1800s (the nineteenth century), the education of all children began to be taken seriously for the first time. It became compulsory for children to go to school from the ages of 5 to 10. It was difficult to enforce this because many poor families needed their children to work, or to look after their younger brothers and sisters while the parents worked.
In 1893, the school leaving age was raised to 11, and in 1899 it was raised again to 12. In 1918, elementary (primary) education became free but children had to go to school until they were 14.
The school leaving age was raised twice more: in 1947 to 15, and in 1972 to 16.

 What do you think the school leaving age should be? Why?

If your family was wealthy, you might still be educated at home with a governess or schoolmaster until you were old enough to be sent to a boarding school.

In the early years of the century most parents had different attitudes to the education of their sons and their daughters. It was thought important for boys to receive a good education because they would have careers and be the breadwinners for their future families.

This is a picture *(right)* of Eton College in Berkshire, England. It was founded in the sixteenth century. Today it can cost thousands of pounds a year for a boy to be a pupil here. It takes only boys. You can find out more on the web site, www.etoncollege.com.

Here is what one woman remembered about being a child in Belfast in the 1920s. "My parents could afford to send only one of us to grammar school. So they sent my brother. I wasn't important enough to educate. They said school would be wasted on me because I would just get married and stay at home to look after children. I have always felt very bad about that; I resented it very much."

Activity

Role-play a discussion between a mother and a father in 1925. They have a son and a daughter. What arguments will they put forward when deciding on the education of their children?

Right up until the 1960s most children lived in families where there was only one income. Their father would go out to work and their mother would be at home to look after them and to run the house.

What do you think of a lifestyle like this?
What is good about it for (a) the children (b) the mother (c) the father?
Are there any disadvantages for (a) the children (b) the mother (c) the father?

Peggy Cairns recalled what happened when she became engaged to be married in 1945. "I was working as a telephonist in Belfast. I had to give up my job because where I worked, women weren't allowed to stay on after they got married."

Women having to leave work when they got married wasn't the case everywhere, but many people – both men and women – supported the idea of married women staying at home. What arguments do you think they put forward in support of this attitude?

National Schools

In 1832, the government set up National Schools in Ireland. There was no other system like this in the rest of the UK. They were for primary age children and still existed at the beginning of the twentieth century. Around the time of the First World War they were becoming known as **Public Elementary Schools**. These schools improved the level of education in Ireland and many more children were able to read and write.

You can still see the remains of National Schools in the countryside. The picture on the next page shows one at Derriaghy, near Lisburn, Co Antrim. The plaque in the middle under the roof gives the name of the school and when it was built.

As you travel about, you could see if you can spot the remains of other National Schools. There were many of them built.

In the earliest schools, hygiene wasn't a top priority — the toilet might be quite a distance away from the school building and was just a shed with a seat with a hole in it!

Children of different ages were taught in the one classroom, by one teacher. The teacher would give the older ones something to do while she taught the younger ones and then they swopped over.

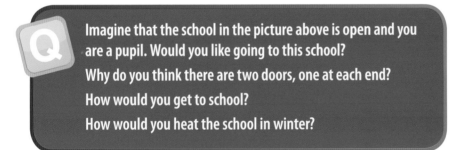

Q Imagine that the school in the picture above is open and you are a pupil. Would you like going to this school?

Why do you think there are two doors, one at each end?

How would you get to school?

How would you heat the school in winter?

 TPD
BC

 LINK TO TRANSPORT 1

Right up until the 1950s, in some schools in rural areas children wrote on slates with chalk. They didn't have exercise books. When you had to do sums or write something, there would be a race to get the best slate because often they got broken or cracked!

The teacher would write with chalk on a blackboard which was cleaned with a felt duster. The duster had a wooden back to hold it by. Every pupil wanted to get picked to clean the duster. The teacher would send the pupil outside with the duster and a ruler and the child beat the felt with the ruler. Chalk dust went everywhere!

School desks had circular holes for inserting an inkwell. One of the jobs a pupil did was to go round in the morning with a big bottle of ink and fill the inkwells. To make the ink go further it could be diluted with water.

These inkwells spilled easily and on very old school desks you can still see the stains. It was also very easy to flick ink at someone you didn't like!

A chalkboard duster with chalk and a pen with a nib.

RURAL: the countryside, not the town.

Activity

Here is a photograph of a classroom around 1900. Look at it carefully and describe what you see.

Talk about each item in the room.

Do you know what the frame in the corner is?

Can you see the holes for inkwells in the desks?

What do you think the bottles on the window sill could be?

What would it be like to have lessons in this room?

What is the modern equivalent of each of the items in the room?

What is different about your classroom compared to the one on the picture?

Is anything the same?

You can see real classrooms from the past in the Ulster-American Folk Park near Omagh in Co Tyrone and at the Ulster Folk Museum at Cultra, near Belfast.

Teachers concentrated on reading, writing and arithmetic. Discipline was very strict. Children could get smacked and even be caned, not just for bad behaviour but also if they got their spellings or sums wrong.

All mathematics were either worked out in your head or by doing sums on a counting frame, slate or paper. There were no calculators in classrooms until the 1990s.

This is a page from a copy book. Pupils had to copy the writing given.

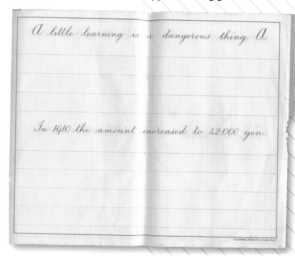

Activity

See how you would have got on in a maths lesson in 1900!
Do these sums in your head:

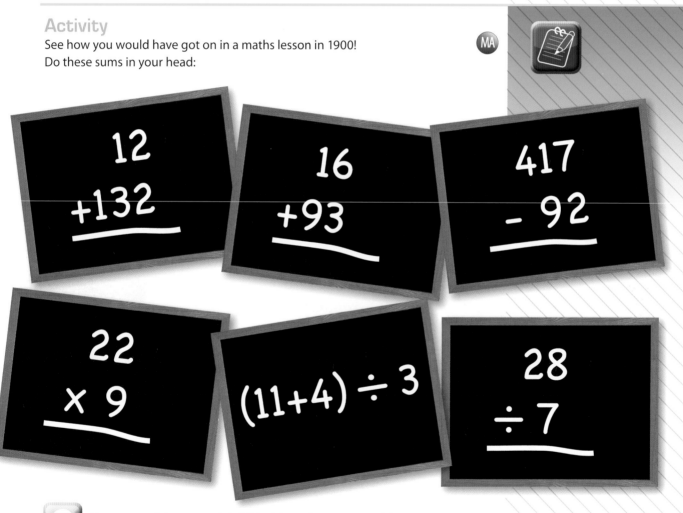

12
+132

16
+93

417
- 92

22
× 9

(11+4) ÷ 3

28
÷ 7

 How many did you get right? Would you have got a gold star or would you have been smacked?

 Are you happy with the number you got right or do you think you need to get a bit better at mental arithmetic?

During the second half of the twentieth century many small country schools closed. Children go to bigger schools now. Why do you think this has happened?

Activity

Imagine you are eight years old and you have just been told that your little school four fields away, with thirty pupils of all ages, is going to be closed down. You are going to have to go to a bigger school in the nearest town.

How will this change affect: you?
your teacher?
what friends you have?
your home and family?
the community where you live?

Did you know there were no **teddy bears** until 1902?

The first jointed soft bear was designed by a German called **Richard Steiff**. He worked in his aunt's toy manufacturing business. There was a zoo nearby and he loved to go to watch and sketch the bears. In 1902 the Steiff firm made their first bear, based on Richard Steiff's drawings.

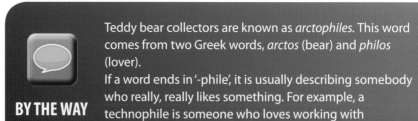

BY THE WAY

Teddy bear collectors are known as *arctophiles*. This word comes from two Greek words, *arctos* (bear) and *philos* (lover).
If a word ends in '-phile', it is usually describing somebody who really, really likes something. For example, a technophile is someone who loves working with technology. A Francophile loves all things French.
If a word ends in '-phobe' it means the opposite. For example, a technophobe strongly *dislikes* technology, and a Francophobe hates anything to do with France!

Meanwhile, the President of the United States was Theodore Roosevelt. His nickname was 'Teddy'. One day he was out hunting and hadn't managed to shoot anything. His attendants captured a bear cub and tied it up for him to shoot but Roosevelt refused to shoot a captured animal. A cartoonist called Clifford Berryman drew a cartoon that appeared in *The Washington Post* newspaper in November 1902.

 The cartoon shows the incident.

Who are the people in the cartoon?

What words would you use to describe the way each of the men is feeling?

How does the cartoonist want you to feel about the bear cub? How does he make you feel this?

If you were Roosevelt, would you have shot the bear? Why or why not?

Soon cute toys called 'Teddy's Bears' were being manufactured and there was a real craze for them. Steiff's bears were developed in Germany quite separately, but soon they were being called teddy bears too.

Stories for children were written, featuring teddy bears. Here is a book featuring **Rupert the Bear.**

 Q **Can you think of any other famous bears in stories?**

Germany had a large toy industry and very many of the toys in the UK came from there at the beginning of the century. They became cheap enough for more parents to be able to buy their child a teddy bear.
The United States made many toys too, but it was such a big country that almost all that it produced was sold at home.

The First World War affected so much of ordinary life and it even affected children's toys. In 1914 war broke out and Britain was at war with Germany. The government banned all imports from Germany. Cross-Atlantic travel became more dangerous so no toys could come from America either. This meant that British firms were able to develop their own toy factories without any competition from abroad. Also, workshops were set up to give employment to disabled servicemen returning from the war. Many of these included toys in their products.

LINK TO FIRST WORLD WAR UNIT

LINK TO MONEY UNIT

One of the most popular toys was invented by **Frank Hornby** in 1901 – **Meccano**. This was a construction toy made of metal. Hornby was a train engineer and he made the bits to enable children to learn about engineering. Children loved it and different sets were made. You could move from a Number 2 set to a Number 3 set and so on. In 1912, Hornby brought out a Meccano magazine, which was published right up to 1981. It cost one penny, in old money. In later years the price went up and it covered all sorts of hobbies, not just Meccano.

A gearbox made from Meccano

Fig. 2. The pre-selector gear-box seen from the other side, with part of the casing removed.

Activity

1   Why do you think Hornby brought out a Meccano magazine?

Make a list of possible contents for a magazine for children following a hobby such as Meccano. Remember that you want children to keep buying the magazine so you have to make it interesting to them.

2   Meccano magazine was aimed exclusively at boys. Why do you think this was?

Many games that children played were the same games that Victorian children played before them. Here are some of them.

Blind Man's Buff

One person is blindfolded and has to catch one of the others. If the blindfolded person catches someone, he has to identify them. If he can't, he has to let them go and try again. If he knows who it is, that person becomes the blindfolded person.

Hunt the Slipper

Children sit in a circle on the floor and one person stands in the middle. He or she is the Hunter. A slipper is passed round the circle very fast and as secretly as possible. The Hunter has to tap the person who has the slipper before they can pass it on. Sometimes a thimble or a marble was used instead because it was easier to pass round without being seen.

Burn the biscuit

One person leaves the room and something small, such as a threepenny bit or a thimble is hidden in the room. The person outside is brought in and he or she has to find it. If they find it they get a turn to hide it. If not, they have to go out of the room and try again.

LINK TO MONEY UNIT

Some families still play these games. You could have a go at one of them at home.

There weren't so many cars on the roads in the first half of the century. There were horse-drawn vehicles but they didn't travel fast so it was much safer for children to play on the streets.

Q Here are some children playing in a street in Belfast in the 1940s. How different do you think this street looks nowadays?

Girls sometimes tied ropes to the tops of the gas streetlamps and swung from them, going round and round the pole. If you didn't go fast enough, you would drop towards the pole and bang your head!

Activity

Imagine you are a 10-year-old child from 1925 who is able to time-travel to today. Write a letter to your parents who are still back in 1925, telling them about playing with children today. What do you find new or strange? Is anything unchanged?

Several games, which are very familiar to us now, were invented in the twentieth century.

Monopoly

OILCLOTH: a cloth that has been made waterproof.

LINK TO MONEY UNIT

The Great Depression of the 1930s in the United States was responsible for the invention of one of the most popular games in the world.

Charles Darrow (1889 – 1967) of Philadelphia had lost his job and was very short of money, like so many people at that time. He decided to do something about it. On an oilcloth on his kitchen table he drew out an idea for a game board. He typed up some rules and title deeds and made little houses and hotels from scrap wood. He used the street names of Atlantic City in New Jersey for his original idea. The game was so successful that he sold the rights to a company who mass-produced it. It arrived in the UK in 1936. Charles Darrow went from being out of work to being a millionaire.

Monopoly is sold all over the world now, and the streets of many cities feature as the properties to buy and sell. There is a Northern Ireland version of Monopoly.

TIP

PROJECT

BEFORE YOU
START

ACTIVITY

BY THE WAY

SOURCES

WORD BOX

LINK

RESEARCH

Activity

Divide into groups and see if your group can invent a board game. The catch is that it has to be a game that could have been manufactured and played in 1910! So you can't use plastic or batteries. You can use wood, cardboard and paper. Anything that moves has to be clockwork. You can't have ballpens to write down the scores either.

BALLOT: when people vote, such as in a political selection.

Each group has to play their game in front of the rest of the class. Then the class should hold a secret ballot on which is the best game. Have a prize for the winning group.

Secret ballots are used for many things such as political elections. Why do you think most ballots are secret?

BY THE WAY

The first successful ball point pen was made by László Bíró, a Hungarian newspaper editor. He was fed up filling his fountain pens with ink and having smudges on his pages. The fountain pen nib also made holes in the newspaper. Bíró and his brother George began to work on designing a new type of pen. Bíró fitted a tiny ball at the tip of the pen. As the pen was moved along the paper, the ball rotated picking up ink from inside the pen and leaving lines on the paper. Bíró patented his invention in 1938.

Because of this invention, what do school desks not have now?

Lego

A Danish carpenter called Ole Kirk Christiansen began making wooden toys in 1932. By 1934 his company was called Lego. This name comes from two Danish words *leg godt*, which mean 'play well'.

Lego bricks weren't invented just as we see them today. The first Lego bricks were like traditional bricks, meant to be placed one on top of the other. By 1949, the company had developed the interlocking system, with studs on top of the bricks which could be snapped together and taken apart easily. They were called 'Automatic Binding Bricks'

Modern Lego that we see today was developed by 1958. If you had a Lego piece from 1958, it would fit a piece that was made today.

A survey by the Victoria and Albert Museum of Childhood found that Lego is the most popular toy of the last 100 years.

The manufacturers of Lego could have kept producing their original bricks. Why do you think they kept looking at how to develop and change them? What would happen if they didn't change them as time went on?

Research

Find out as much as you can about Rubik's Cube.
Present your findings in summary form using bullet points.
Format your summary like this:

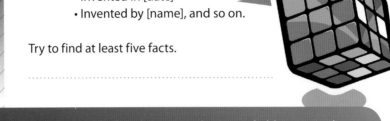

- Invented in [date]
- Invented by [name], and so on.

Try to find at least five facts.

BY THE WAY

It is possible that the yoyo is the second oldest toy in the world. It is thought to have been used in China about 1000BC. Ivory was used for the disks and the string was made of silk. The one in the picture dates from the beginning of the twentieth century. The earliest yoyos which have been found were made about 500BC. The oldest toy is the doll.
If the earliest yoyos found so far date from around 500BC, how do historians know that there may have been yoyos in 1000BC?

Sweets

Many of the sweets and chocolates that you know today were introduced in the twentieth century. In the early 1900s, sweets were a luxury but from the 1920s more and more were made. During the Second World War, sweets were rationed and even after the war ended in 1945 they were still rationed until 1953.

Activity

With a partner, choose one of the following items of confectionery and find out as much as you can about its history. Report your findings to the class.

Crunchie
Milky Way
Maltesers
KitKat
Smarties
Rolo
Bounty
Mars Bar
Aero
Polo Mints
Fry's Chocolate Cream
Liquorice Allsorts
Love Hearts
Rowntree's Fruit Pastilles

Evacuees during the Second World War

During the Second World War (1939–45) there was great danger from the German airforce, the Luftwaffe, which bombed cities in Britain and Northern Ireland. The government became concerned for the safety of children and ordered them to be evacuated to the county.

Activity

Look at this picture.

EVACUATED: sent away.

A soldier is kissing his little son goodbye at the train station as children are evacuated out of London and other cities that might be vulnerable to attack. The box on the little boy's back contains his gas mask. Everyone was given a gas mask to carry in case the enemy launched a poison gas attack.

What is the mood of this picture?
What words would you use to describe it?
How do you think the children are feeling?
Describe the emotions of the father.

Activity

1. Imagine you are an evacuee. You are in a strange house, with a strange family after a long day travelling by train to a country village that you have never been in before. You have come from a small house in a city street.

   Write a diary entry just before you go to bed. Explain, just for yourself, all that has happened and how you feel about it. How do your surroundings differ from the surroundings you are used to?

2. It is four weeks later. Write another diary entry. What has changed? How do you feel now? Have you discovered anything interesting about the countryside? Do you want to stay here or do you want to go back home?

Research

Here are three children who were famous in the twentieth century.

Anastasia, youngest daughter of Tsar Nicholas II of Russia

Anne Frank, a Jewish girl in the Second World War

Research the life of one of these people. Write a short account of the historical events in which this child was involved.

You could also:
- create a wall display
- write a five minute drama of a scene from the person's life

Pu Yi (Pǔyí) the last Emperor of China

TIP

PROJECT

BEFORE YOU START

ACTIVITY

BY THE WAY

SOURCES

WORD BOX

LINK

RESEARCH

Research

Research the history of your school.

Find out:
• when it was founded
• if it was always on the site it is on now
• who could attend it at the beginning
• whether there have been any extensions or renovations
• the names of all the headmasters or headmistresses
• whether any famous people were pupils of your school in the past
• any other facts or stories you discover

Collect any photographs or illustrations which show your school in the past. Maybe there are pictures of sports teams or prize days.

Present your findings as a portfolio of information.

Perhaps as a class you could make a major display on the history of your school for a school notice board.

Class Quiz!

Divide into two teams and decide on a prize for the winning team If you get a question right, your team gets a point, BUT if you get a question wrong, you lose a point! So think carefully before you answer!

1. What is 28 divided by 7?
2. What is 'Burn the Biscuit'?
3. Name four basic human needs.
4. What is the word 'pram' short for?
5. When was Edward VII king?
6. In what year was the National Health Service introduced?
7. What is the long name for a collector of teddy bears?
8. What was the Family Allowance?
9. Who set up a Ragged School in 1867?
10. When was your school first opened?
11. Why is Dr Benjamin Spock famous?
12. Which newspaper published the cartoon of Roosevelt and the bear cub?
13. In what year was the school leaving age raised to 15?
14. Name one child who was part of a major historical event.
15. What is a paediatrician?
16. What was the name of the schools set up in Ireland in 1832?
17. What did pupils write on if there were no exercise books?
18. How did teddy bears get their name?
19. Who was the German toy-maker who made the first teddy bear?
20. What city featured in the very first Monopoly game?

Your Timeline

Draw a timeline and mark on it all the dates that you have read about in this chapter and what happened on those dates.

Word Check

Check out these words to make sure you can spell them.

evacuate	**portfolio**	**government**
ration	**vehicle**	**automatic**
century	**blindfold**	**chocolate**
elementary	**biscuit**	**original**
confectionery	**sympathetic**	**hygiene**
millionaire	**national**	**Berkshire**
Philadelphia	**community**	

If you're not sure if you can spell any of them, check them out a few more times.

Review this Unit

Have a class discussion on what you have learnt in this Unit.
Share with the class things that you found particularly interesting.
Was there anything that surprised you?
Is there anything more you would like to know? If so, how would you find out about it?

TIP

PROJECT

BEFORE YOU START

ACTIVITY

BY THE WAY

SOURCES

WORD BOX

LINK

RESEARCH

MEDICINE

Has anyone in your class had the experience of being in hospital?
Perhaps someone in your class knows someone who has been in hospital.
Only if they would like to, perhaps they could share this experience with the class.
What were the doctors and nurses like? What was the ward like? How long was it necessary to stay in hospital?

BEFORE YOU START

Activity

Now look at this picture. It shows a hospital ward in 1900.

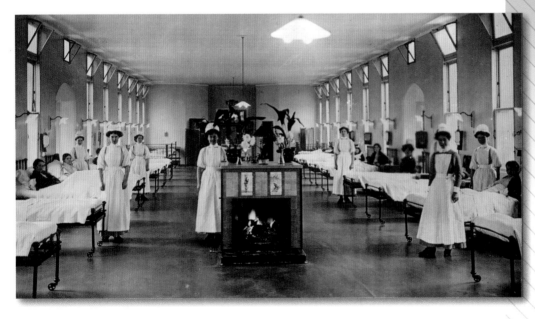

Talk about this picture. What do you see?

Does it look anything like our hospital wards today?

Would you like to be a patient in this ward? Do you need to know more about it in order to form an opinion? What more would you like to know?

Would you like to be a nurse in this ward?

What do you think of the uniforms?

Compare it to a hospital ward today. Write out two lists – one for things that are the same and one for things that are different.

If you could talk to one of these nurses, what would you ask her?

There were many important developments in medicine in the twentieth century. At the beginning of the century, average life expectancy in the UK was 47 years. By the year 2000 it was 77 years. We will explore how this big improvement came about.

Q Think about what an 'average' is. Explain it to a partner.
Now think about this. There were plenty of people over 70 years old in 1900, although not nearly as many as there are now. So why do you think the average life expectancy was only 47? What could be bringing the average down?

Discuss with a partner why people didn't live as long as they do now.

Work out the average age of your family. Include grandparents if possible.

BY THE WAY

Doctors in hospitals often have a stethoscope round their necks. This is used for listening to the workings of organs in the body to see if they are healthy, eg the heart and lungs. The stethoscope was invented in 1816 by a French doctor called Laënnec. His first one was just a pile of paper rolled into a tube. One end was put on the patient's chest and the doctor put his ear to the other end. Better ones were developed and now most of them have two earpieces.

Try this at home!

Make your own single earpiece stethoscope.

You will need two ordinary plastic kitchen funnels. The wide opening shouldn't be more than about 7 cms in diameter. The narrow spout should be about 1 cm in diameter.
You will also need a piece of tubing about 45 cms long and narrow enough to fit over the narrow end of each funnel.
Fit a funnel into each end of the tube.
Put one end of your 'stethoscope' to your ear and the other end over your heart. It might need to be quiet for you to hear anything!
Notice how the heart sounds and the speed of the beats.
Try running on the spot for five minutes and then listen to your heart again. Does it sound different?

One of the most important developments which transformed the world of medicine in general and surgery in particular was the realisation that a lack of cleanliness made it much more likely that wounds would become infected. Up until nearly the end of the nineteenth century, hospitals and operating rooms could be filthy!

Imagine if you were going for an operation and the surgeon strolled in to the operating theatre straight from lunch and didn't even wash his hands. The surgical instruments might fall on the floor or a nurse might sneeze over them, but they carried on using them anyway.

Patients could survive an operation well, but then die from an infection that set in after it.

TRANSFORMED: changed a lot

SWABBED: wiped with a damp cloth or sponge

GANGRENE: where flesh dies off because of a lack of blood supply

Joseph Lister discovered how to stop germs from leading to infections and gangrene. He discovered that if wounds were swabbed with carbolic acid they stayed much cleaner and the patient was much more likely to get better. He also made surgeons wear rubber gloves during surgery and wash their hands in a solution of carbolic acid. Surgical instruments were sterilised too.

 Joseph Lister is often called the 'father of modern antiseptics'. There is a product you can buy in a chemist's shop today that is name after Lister. Can you think what it is?

When Edward VII came to the throne in 1901, he came down with appendicitis two days before his coronation. Lister was so important to medicine at that time that the surgeons consulted him before they would operate on the king! After he had recovered, the king said to Lister "I know that if it had not been for you and your work, I wouldn't be sitting here today".

 Who was Edward VII's mother?

 Do you think that surgeons in the nineteenth century were very stupid not to realise the importance of cleanliness? Explain your opinion.

War and Medicine

It might seem strange, but wars can give rise to new developments in medicine. People are wounded in wartime and they need to be cared for.

The Lady with the Lamp

Back in the nineteenth century, there was a nurse who became famous for her work with the wounded in the Crimean War (1853–1856). She was called **Florence Nightingale.** She lived from 1820 to 1910.

What age was she when she died?

In the Crimea, she set up **field hospitals.** These are hospitals that are set up close to the fighting. There were field hospitals during wars in the twentieth century, for example in Vietnam. There was a TV series called M.A.S.H. It was a fictional story of doctors working in a field hospital during the Korean War.

M.A.S.H. is an **acronym** for Mobile Army Surgical Hospital.

Do you know any other acronyms? For example, NATO stands for **N**orth **A**tlantic **T**reaty **O**rganisation.

See how many you can think of.

LINK TO 1st WORLD WAR UNIT

This is a drawing of one of the wards in the hospital that Florence Nightingale set up at Scutari in the Crimea.

What words would you use to describe how this ward looks?

How do you imagine this ward feels? Does it seem as if the patients are well cared for or are they neglected? What evidence is there to support your opinion?

Find out where the Crimea is.

Florence Nightingale is so famous that her portrait was on Bank of England £10 notes which were issued from 1975 to 1994.

Her work in the Crimea was described in a report in the *London Times* newspaper while she was alive:

"She is a 'ministering angel' without any exaggeration in these hospitals, and as her slender form glides quietly along each corridor, every poor fellow's face softens with gratitude at the sight of her. When all the medical officers have

LINK TO MONEY UNIT

retired for the night and silence and darkness have settled down upon those miles of prostrate sick, she may be observed alone, with a little lamp in her hand, making her solitary rounds."

PROSTRATE: lying flat
SOLITARY: alone

Activity

Do you think the writer from the *London Times* admired Nightingale? Give evidence from the newspaper report to support your opinion.
Imagine you are a reporter and you don't like Nightingale. Rewrite this report differently to try to make readers dislike her. You mustn't actually *say* you don't like her or her work. You must change some words to make readers *feel* you don't like her.

One of the great problems which injured soldiers faced was infection and gangrene. Nowadays, someone with a leg wound could be cured completely, but during the First World War the leg might become so infected that it would have to be amputated. There were no anaesthetics then such as the ones we have now, so the leg might have to be cut off while the patient was awake!
So many men were dying in great pain that doctors and nurses did their best to find cures. There was also a more practical reason. Governments could not afford to lose so many soldiers. They were needed to fight.

Penicillin

Did you know that in 1900 you could die as a result of getting a scratch on your finger? This was because bacteria could infect the wound and make you so sick you couldn't get better. When you are sick, does the doctor sometimes prescribe an **antibiotic** to help you get better? This is a medicine that can kill many of the bacteria that are making you sick.

Antibiotics were discovered in the twentieth century and one of the most important of these was **penicillin.**
It was discovered by accident by a scientist called **Alexander Fleming** (1881–1955).
One day in 1928, he was cleaning some of the dishes in his lab when he noticed a mould growing in a petrie dish. He also noticed that, although there were germs in the dish, none of them were able to grow near the mould. He did some experiments and realised that he had discovered an antibiotic that could kill many germs. This was penicillin.
There wasn't enough money available to make much of this discovery at the time. The mould was quite difficult to cultivate and it was hard to extract the penicillin from it.
But when the Second World War broke out in 1939, there were so many wounded soldiers that it became urgent to find ways of making more penicillin to save many lives. Especially when the Americans entered the war after the bombing of **Pearl Harbour** in 1941, more funds were made available for research.
Penicillin was such an important discovery that it is sometimes called 'the miracle drug'.

LINK TO MONEY UNIT

Research

Several organisations work in war-torn areas of the world, to bring help to people affected.

Find the names of at least two of these organisations. Pick one and write an account of its work.

End your account with a paragraph stating your own feelings and opinions on the work of your chosen organisation.

TPD

SM

Class Discussion

We go to the doctor to get a prescription for an antibiotic if we need it. We don't have to worry about getting really ill from an infected cut on a finger.

You have seen that money is needed to fund research to develop medicines.

Imagine that you live in a poor country in Africa.

How would you feel if your brother or sister or someone else whom you loved, was dying and you knew that an antibiotic could cure them? The country where you live is not buying any medicine for its people. It is spending all its money on fighting a war instead. Your family is poor and can't afford to bring the sick person to another country where they might be cured.

Talk about this in class for a few minutes.
What could you do to help the sick person?
What emotions would you experience?

Do you think it is fair that you are able to get medicine when you need it and other people in the world can't? Justify your opinion.

The Guinea Pig Club

There was another great advance in medicine because of the Second World War. Fighter planes were not as sophisticated then as they are now. It was very dangerous to be a fighter pilot.

The Battle of Britain was fought in the air over south-eastern England in 1940. Adolf Hitler, the German Führer, wanted to wipe out the British air force so that Britain would be much easier to invade. Many pilots were killed or severely burned. Those who survived were often horribly disfigured.

Plastic surgery was just beginning to be carried out at this time. A surgeon called **Archibald McIndoe** (left) realised that he could use his skill to try to help these men recover and feel that they could lead normal lives again.

At the Queen Victoria Cottage Hospital in East Grinstead in the south of England, he used various experimental methods of reconstructing the men's faces and limbs. In this way, the skill of plastic surgery developed and we still benefit from McIndoe's work today.

He found that the wounds of pilots who had been shot down into the sea recovered more quickly than those of pilots who had crashed on land. He realised that it had something to do with the salt water, so he used saline baths to help heal wounds.

His patients got together and called themselves The Guinea Pig Club.

LINK TO WAR UNIT

RECONSTRUCTING: making again

SALINE: containing salt

Q Was this a good name? Why do you think this?

McIndoe didn't just try to fix their terrible injuries. He also wanted them to get better mentally. He encouraged the men to go into the town and get used to people looking at them. He allowed them to wear their own clothes and not hospital clothes.

Activity

You are a pilot who was shot down over the English Channel during the Battle of Britain. The fuel tanks in your fighter plane exploded as you were trying to get out of the cockpit. You have been taken to Dr McIndoe's hospital and you will have to undergo several plastic surgery operations on your face.

Write a diary entry recording what has happened and how you feel. It's your diary so you can be very honest. Think about:

- how you feel about having wounds to your face

- whether you are scared of what the operations will involve

- what you feel about the war. Have your views changed?

- what it's like in the hospital

When you have finished, perhaps the teacher could ask some of you to read out your accounts. You could talk about them.

Activity

You have finished your diary entry and now you have to write a letter to your parents to tell them what has happened and where you are.

You don't want to worry your parents too much but you do want them to know that you are injured. How will you say it? Will you use different words in your letter to the ones you used in your diary?

Activity

If you had been able to text a mate in the Air Force about what has happened to you, what would you have typed in your message? You have a maximum of 400 letters and spaces.

The National Health Service

Ordinary people had made many sacrifices during the war. There was a feeling that people now deserved a better, fairer country. In fact, during the war, a man called **William Beveridge** was asked to produce a report on the social conditions of the ordinary people so that the country could be rebuilt after the war. In 1942, he produced **The Beveridge Report.** One of his main recommendations was that there should be a National Health Service so people would get free medical care.

Before this, most people had to pay for their medical care. If you needed to see a doctor or needed an operation, your family had to pay for it. If you could not pay, you did not get any medical help.

Clement Atlee became Labour Prime Minister in 1945, the year the Second World War ended. **Aneurin** (pronounced 'An-iron') **Bevan** was the Minister for Health in Atlee's government and he implemented Beveridge's recommendation and set up the National Health Service in 1948.

 Q The NHS celebrated its anniversary in 2008. What anniversary was it?

POULTICE: a hot, moist bundle of cloth containing herbs, which was placed on a sore or wounded part of the body to help it heal.

Here are comments from two people about the NHS.

Betty is 84 and well remembers the days before the NHS when a visit from the doctor would cost half a crown [12.5p] – a sizeable part of the weekly budget. "You didn't get the doctor unless you could really help it. My grandmother had all sorts of remedies – she would slap a poultice on your chest to stop you coughing. That's what things were like back then."

SM

Damien is a 35 year old civil servant. He say: "The NHS is the single greatest achievement of British democracy. My mother spent her entire working life as a nurse, midwife and health visitor in the NHS. It is only people of my mother's generation and older who remember life before. They seem to value it more than anybody else but the future of the NHS is in the hands of younger tax payers. They should speak to their parents."

TPD

Q Opinion time!

Do you think we take the NHS for granted today?

Do you agree with Damien that "The NHS is the single greatest achievement of British democracy"?

"Because of the NHS we are all softies now and we've forgotten how to use natural remedies." Do you agree with this statement? Give your reasons.

In groups consider this question:

Should people pay for medical treatment if they can afford it?

To form an opinion on this, you need to look at the arguments for and against. As you think about this, remember what you have learnt about medical treatment in the past. Draw a table like the following on a page of your notebook.

Rich should pay for medical treatment because	Medical treatment should be free for everyone because

1. In each column put reasons in favour of each statement.

2. When you have thought of as many reasons as you can, put them in order of importance. You will need to discuss each one within your group.

   Are there different viewpoints? If so, you must listen to all of the viewpoints and come to an agreed decision. If you decide one reason is the most important one, rank it as number 1, and so on.

3. Compare your list with the other groups. Appoint one person from each group to explain why you have rank ordered your reasons the way you have.

4. When you have finished, consider your findings. Are there more arguments in favour of free health care or against it?

5. Come to a conclusion. Complete the sentence: "We believe that health care should …"

6. Is there anyone in your group who does *not* agree with the findings of the group? If so, *someone else* in the same group must explain to the class why their classmate does *not* agree.

BY THE WAY

James Miranda Barry was a surgeon in the British Army. He lived from about 1792 to 1865 and worked in both India and South Africa. He was very much respected for his skill and became Inspector General in charge of military hospitals. After he died it was discovered that he was – a woman!

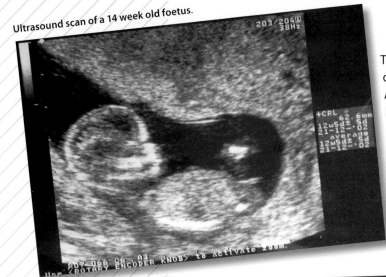
Ultrasound scan of a 14 week old foetus.

There were many other medical inventions and discoveries in the twentieth century.

At the end of the nineteenth century, **Wilhelm Roentgen** had discovered X-Rays. Now we have ultrasound scans, magnetic resonance imaging (MRI) and computer tomography (CT) scans.

All these techniques help doctors to see inside the patient's body to find out what may be making the person ill.

Try this!

Stand and raise one hand high above your head, straight up in the air.

Keep your other hand hanging down by your side.

Stand like this for several minutes.

Then put your two hands side by side in front of you, palms facing down. Are your hands different colours? Why do you think this is?

Transplant surgery

In the second half of the twentieth century, it became possible to get spare parts for your body! Many organs can be transplanted, including the liver and kidneys. The first person to perform a heart transplant was a South African surgeon called **Christian Barnard.** This took place in 1967.

Find out if this operation was successful.

Think about organ transplants. What usually has to happen in order to find a new organ for a sick person?
Do you agree with transplanting organs?
Would you donate one of your organs?
People who are willing to do so may carry the organ donor card.

Many people join the online Organ Donor Register. You can find out more about organ donation at www.uktransplant.org./uk/ukt.

As well as being able to transplant organs, doctors discovered how to make artificial organs. One of the most common operations, specially for older people, is to replace a hip joint which may become very sore as the joint ages. Knees and elbows can also be replaced by artificial ones.

Project

You are going to examine attitudes to disability in the twentieth century.

Read the following descriptions of two people who suffered from disability. The first person was rarely seen in public and the second person was very famous indeed.

1. The Lost Prince

You may have read about Edward VIII elsewhere in this book. He was the king who abdicated because he wanted to marry a divorced American woman.

Edward VIII had a younger brother, Prince John, who was rarely seen in public and died in 1919 when he was only 13 years old. He suffered severely with epilepsy at a time when there was no medication to treat it, as there is today.

At that time, at the beginning of the twentieth century, people with disabilities were regarded as an embarrassment to the family. They were hidden away and never talked about. Often they were put into institutions where other disabled people were kept.

Because Prince John's parents were the king and queen, George V and Queen Mary, he was able to stay in a house on a royal estate and be looked after by a nanny.

If Prince John had to go to London to see doctors, the windows of the car had the blinds drawn in case he was seen having an epileptic fit.

The doctor recorded the death of Prince John in these words:

"HRH Prince John, who has since infancy suffered from epileptic fits, which have lately become more frequent and severe, passed away in his sleep following an attack this afternoon at Sandringham."

Prince John is buried in the churchyard at Sandringham. The inscription reads: "HRH Prince John, 1905–1919."

 LINK TO MONEY UNIT

 PARALYSIS: a loss of the ability to move

2. President Franklin D Roosevelt

One of the terrible diseases that people suffered from was polio. It was particularly common in Britain, Ireland and America in the first half of the twentieth century. Most, but not all, of those who contracted it were children.

Polio is caused by a virus that attacks the nervous system and can leave the sufferer with permanent paralysis. There was an epidemic of polio in Ireland from about 1947 to 1957.

Franklin D Roosevelt was one of the most famous people to contract polio. He became ill in 1921 when he was 39 years old.

After his illness he went on to be elected President of the United States from 1933–1945.

With the help of his family and staff, Roosevelt tried very hard not to let people

see how disabled he was. There are only two family photographs of him in a wheelchair. (You can see one of these on the left.) He could walk with the help of special supports on his legs, called 'callipers' or 'braces'.

These are some of the ways he hid his walking difficulty:

- The lower end of his callipers were painted black so that they did not show up too much.
- His trousers were cut very long to cover the callipers as much as possible.
- When he was giving a speech, he always sat as close to the podium as possible.
- He walked slowly with the aid of a stick and often leaned on the arm of his son.
- He could stand gripping a podium to make a speech, but the podium was always securely bolted to the ground.
- When he was at dinners or state functions, he was seated already when the others came in.
- He was never lifted in public and was never seen in a wheelchair in public.

The newspapers of the time knew all about Roosevelt's difficulties but they didn't report it. By not doing so they helped him to hide his disability.

1 Divide into groups and decide what you want to do with this information.

You could write and produce a short scene where King George V and Queen Mary have realised that their son has epilepsy. They are discussing what to do with him. It would be a good idea to research some more information about Prince John before you write your scene.

- What factors do his parents have to consider?
- What are the possible courses of action for them?
- What do you think they are feeling at this time?
- Are the King and Queen's feelings the same or do you think they might look at the situation differently?

Try to express as much as you can through your characters and what they say. You don't have to have only two characters. There may have been courtiers and even John's other brothers involved.

2

You could produce a display for the classroom on the history of polio in the twentieth century. Examine questions like these:

- What caused it?
- How was it treated by doctors?
- Did treatment change during the course of the century?
- Were there any inventions which helped patients to recover?
- Why don't people get polio in this country now?

Can people living in some other countries still get polio? Explain why this is.

Could you interview someone who had polio?

Here are some useful web sites:

Polio Fellowship of Northern Ireland   www.polio-ni.org/

British Polio Organisation   www.britishpolio.org.uk/default.aspx

Post Polio Support Group Ireland   www.ppsg.ie

 3

You could put together an IT presentation to the class on attitudes to disability in the twentieth century. Remember that there are many different sorts of disability.

Meet as a group and decide what way you will structure your report. Everyone must contribute something. Plan how you will deliver your presentation. Will you use Powerpoint or some other software?

Give everyone one aspect to research.

You could give case histories of Prince John and President Roosevelt and say what were the main reactions to them. One was a child and one was an adult. Do you think this made a difference to how they were treated? Explain this in your presentation.

Give reasons why President Roosevelt felt that he had to disguise his disability as much as he could.

 COM

 ICT

 MI

 TPD

 WO

Change over time

Look at how disabled people are treated today. Investigate some modern examples of disability and show how differently society responds now.
How has the law changed? What facilities must be available for disabled people?

Review your work

Do you think your group worked well together? Why or why not?

Were you pleased with your finished work?

What two things did you do really well?

What do you think you could have done better?

Now complete this sentence: "By doing this task, I have learned …"

Is anyone in your class a wheelchair user? If so, he or she will find this task very easy.

Your task is to spend one day at home as if you had to use a wheelchair.

You must stop at any obstruction that is higher than 2 cms and work out how you could get past it.

You must notice doorways – are they wide enough for your wheelchair? Can you reach the door handles and have you enough strength to open them? If not, what can you do? What if the door opens towards you?

How do you carry stuff ?

How do you go out to the shops or a friend's house?

Make notes as you go along and discuss your experience when you come back to class.

What have you noticed? Did you notice things that you didn't think of before?

On a scale of 1 to 10, how disability friendly is your home (10 is excellent, 1 is hopeless).

What would need to be done to your house if one of your family was a wheelchair user?

What would be more difficult for a wheelchair user in 1910?

Class Quiz!

Divide into two teams and decide on a prize for the winning team. If you get a question right, your team gets a point, BUT if you get a question wrong, you lose a point!

1. What was the average life expectancy at the beginning of the twentieth century?
2. Doctors often carry something round their necks to listen to a patient's heart and lungs. What is it called?
3. What did Joseph Lister discover?
4. Who discovered penicillin?
5. After what major bombing event did the Americans enter the Second World War?
6. Who was the surgeon who carried out plastic surgery on injured airmen?
7. Who was the Labour Prime Minister when The National Health Service was introduced?
8. What is an acronym?

TIP

PROJECT

BEFORE YOU START

ACTIVITY

BY THE WAY

SOURCES

WORD BOX

LINK

RESEARCH

9. Name two problems faced by injured soldiers in hospital during the First World War.

10. Name the town where Florence Nightingale set up her hospital during the Crimean War.

11. What is the Guinea Pig Club?

12. Who performed the first heart transplant operation?

13. During the Second World War, why did the wounds of pilots who had crashed in the sea heal better than those of pilots who had crashed on land?

14. President Roosevelt went everywhere in a wheelchair. True or false?

Your Timeline

Draw a timeline and mark on it all the dates that you have read about in this chapter and what happened on those dates.

Word Check

Check out these words to make sure you can spell them.

embarrassment
expectancy
stethoscope
realisation
gangrene
acronym
anaesthetic

bacteria
antibiotic
penicillin
prescription
Atlee
Beveridge
disability

Roosevelt
epilepsy
transplant
guinea
diary
medication

If you're not sure if you can spell any of them, check them out a few more times.

BEFORE YOU START

There are 32 counties in Ireland. Close your book and see if your class can name them all.

Which counties are in the province of Ulster?

Ireland in 1900

The people of Ireland had many difficulties during the nineteenth century (1800s). When 1900 arrived, they were leaving behind a century that had seen the terrible famine of the 1840s. Irish people at the time did not feel that the English government had dealt with the famine well and as a result there was a lot of anti-British feeling. This was added to by the Fenian Rising of 1867 and by the Land Wars of 1879–82. You might want to find out more about these events when you have finished this Unit.

Through death and emigration, the population of Ireland in 1900 was just over half the population of a hundred years before. There are many people throughout the world, especially in America and Australia, as well as in Britain, who can trace their family roots back to Ireland.

 CONSTITUTED: made up

Population of selected Irish counties.
Study this table and answer the questions which follow.

Year	Mayo	Louth	Dublin (City and county)	Tipperary	Waterford	Leitrim	Rep of Ireland total	Northern Ireland Total
1841	389,000	128,000	373,000	436,000	196,000	155,000	6529,000	1649,000
1861	255,000	91,000	410,000	249,000	134,000	112,000	4402,000	1396,000
1881	245,000	78,000	419,000	200,000	113,000	90,000	3870,000	1305,000
1901	199,000	66,000	448,000	160,000	87,000	69,000	3222,000	1237,000
1926	173,000	63,000	506,000	141,000	79,000	56,000	2972,000	1257,000
1946	148,000	66,000	636,000	136,000	76,000	45,000	2955,000	1338,000*
1961	123,000	67,000	718,000	124,000	71,000	33,000	2818,000	1425,000
1981	115,000	89,000	1003,000	135,000	89,000	28,000	3443,000	1536,000
1991	110,000	91,000	1025,000	133,000	92,000	25,000	3526,000	1578,000
2006	124,000	111,000	1187,000	149,000	108,000	29,000	4240,000	1685,000**

Figures for Northern Ireland and Republic of Ireland before 1921 are of the counties that later constituted those areas. *Estimate. ** Figure from 2001 census.

1. What factors influence the way population changes?

2. What may have caused population changes in Ireland in the twentieth century?

3. Using the figures in the two right hand columns of the table on the previous page, calculate the total population of Ireland for the years 1841, 1861, 1901 and 1991.

4. Only two counties/cities show a rise in population in 1946. Which are they and what reasons could there be for this?

5. Express the 1901 population figure for the whole island as a percentage of the 1841 population.

6. Plot a graph of the population of the 26 counties of the Republic of Ireland from 1841 to 2006. Then, in a different colour on the same axes, plot a similar graph for the six counties of Northern Ireland. (**Remember** that Northern Ireland and the Republic of Ireland did not exist until 1921. Figures for Northern Ireland and the Republic of Ireland before 1921 are of the counties that later constituted those areas.)

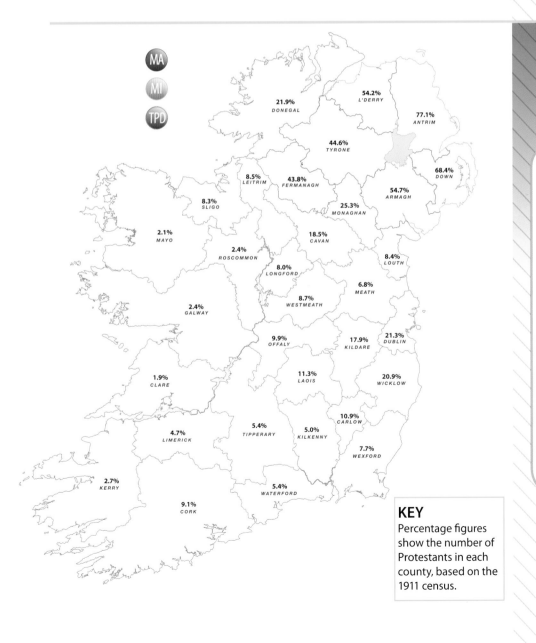

KEY
Percentage figures show the number of Protestants in each county, based on the 1911 census.

Using the percentage figures given for each county, draw a bar chart illustrating the division of Catholics and Protestants in the counties of *either* the whole island of Ireland *or* the province of Ulster.

Now draw a line on a blank map where you think the division of the country could have been best made. Write a statement for the press in which you justify your decision.

Ireland was governed from London. However, there was a Viceroy who represented the sovereign and who lived in Dublin Castle. Queen Victoria paid her last visit to Ireland in 1900. (Do you remember in which year she died? Check on page 5) She was received well by her officials, but her popularity with the ordinary Irish people had diminished greatly.

Left to right: Lord Aberdeen, Queen Mary, King George V, Lady Aberdeen.

DIMINISHED: gone down

King George V and Queen Mary visited Ireland in 1911. Here they are pictured at a garden party given for them by Lord and Lady Aberdeen, at the Viceregal Lodge. Lord Aberdeen was the Viceroy in Ireland at that time.

They are dressed very formally. Why do you think they are dressed like this? Do you think they look as if they are enjoying themselves?

At the end of the nineteenth century the **Gaelic Athletic Association** (GAA) and the **Gaelic League** had been set up. These two organisations worked to increase Irish cultural identity.

Activity

Choose either the GAA *or* the Gaelic League and find out more about them. Half the class should plan an essay on its chosen organisation. First make an outline:

- Decide on your headings. (Always start with 'Introduction' and end with 'Conclusion'.
- Under each heading, note down what you will include.
- Using your outline, write an account of the organisation.

The other half of the class should put together a mark scheme for the essays. Decide what should be included in the essay and how many marks should be given for each point made. Take depth of understanding, spelling and grammar into account. Mark an essay according to your mark scheme and justify the final mark you give.

In 1904, the **Abbey Theatre** was founded in Dublin. This theatre staged plays by Irish playwrights on Irish themes.

As a result of all these movements and events, the early years of the twentieth century saw an increasing sense of Irish identity and a celebration of Ireland's past. John Redmond was the leader of the Irish Parliamentary Party, which wanted Home Rule for Ireland.
In 1905, **Arthur Griffith**, a nationalist, founded the group that was later called Sinn Féin.

These were the aims of Sinn Féin:

1. Ireland to have a parliament of her own in Dublin.
2. The King of England to remain as King of Ireland.
3. An Irish parliament to run the country without English interference.
4. The British government in Ireland would be ignored and wither away.
5. If Ireland was to be really independent, she also had to be economically independent, so people should buy Irish goods, and taxes should be put on foreign goods.

Arthur Griffith

Questions

1. Do any of these aims of Sinn Féin surprise you? If so, which and why?
2. Do you think the fourth aim would have happened in practice?
3. Think through the consequences of the fifth aim. What would be taxed and what would not be taxed? What might other countries do in retaliation?

A Home Rule Bill was debated in the British Parliament three times. The first two times it was defeated, but in 1912, the British Prime Minister, Herbert Asquith, introduced it for the third time.

Class debate

"In the early years of the twentieth century, those who wanted to break the link with Britain were following their hearts rather than their heads." Discuss this statement.

Opposition to Home Rule

There was strong opposition to the idea of Home Rule. This was mostly centred in Ulster, but there was opposition also in the other provinces. The main reasons for wanting to keep the link with Britain were:

• **CULTURAL.** For the Protestant population, Irish culture was too Gaelic. They feared that their own traditions and way of life would be lost.
"We hold that no power, not even the British parliament, has the right to deprive us of our heritage of British citizenship." Bishop D'Arcy of Down, Connor and Dromore.

• **RELIGIOUS.** The majority religion in the island of Ireland was Catholic. Protestants feared that their religious rights would be ignored or even suppressed.
In December 1912, Father Gerald O'Nolan addressed Roman Catholic students at Queen's University, Belfast. He said:
"We shall have a free hand in the future. Let us use it well. This is a Catholic country, and if we do not govern it on Catholic lines, according to Catholic ideals, and to safeguard Catholic interests, it will be all the worse for the country and all the worse for us."

• **ECONOMIC.** For the bigger farmers and for businessmen in Ireland, Britain was an important trading partner. These people feared that breaking the link with Britain would damage Ireland's, and particularly Ulster's, prosperity. Here is the way one person described Belfast:
"By 1914 Belfast could boast 'the greatest shipyard, rope works, tobacco factory, linen mill, dry dock and tea machinery works in the world'. In the late nineteenth and early twentieth centuries Belfast was one of the major industrial powerhouses of the world." From *Celebrating the Ulster Covenant*, Gordon Lucy, The Ulster Society.

SUPPRESS: put down, subdue

 Q Look at the quotations under the headings above. If you were alive in 1912, do you think you would have understood the Unionist position, even if you didn't agree with it?

TIP

PROJECT

BEFORE YOU START

ACTIVITY

BY THE WAY

SOURCES

WORD BOX

LINK

RESEARCH

Sir Edward Carson

The best speaker on the Unionist side was Sir Edward Carson. He set out to use Ulster to block Home Rule. Carson became Unionist leader in 1910. He was a Southern Unionist from Dublin and his home was in London. He was a brilliant public speaker and a very clever leader.

The first chance most Ulster Unionists got to hear Carson was in September 1911 when he spoke to 50,000 Orangemen gathered at Craigavon, Sir James Craig's home, near Belfast. (Don't confuse this with the present town of Craigavon.)

Sir James Craig

Sir James Craig was Carson's deputy. He was a quieter person and a great organiser. He organised a number of mass protest meetings, like the one held at Craigavon in 1911. Although the two men had very different personalities, together they formed a very powerful leadership team which was to direct Ulster Unionist resistance to Home Rule.

Activity

1. In pairs, discuss the two photographs above, of Carson and Craig. Just by looking at them, what would you think their personalities might be? You could write out a list of words to describe them.

2. Taking one each, investigate the life stories of Carson and Craig. Word process a short biography of each one.

3. When you have finished your biographies, discuss whether you were right in what you thought about them when you looked at their photographs.

Protest meetings

Another huge protest meeting was held at Balmoral, which is near Belfast, in April 1912, just two days before Asquith introduced the **Third Home Rule Bill**. A crowd of 100,000 turned out to listen to the Unionist speakers.

So by the summer of 1912 it was clear that if Asquith pushed ahead with the Home Rule Bill, violence could break out in Ulster.

Propaganda

In the struggle over Home Rule both Unionists and Nationalists put forward their own points of view to win support. To influence people they used **propaganda.** Remember that there was no television or radio at this time. This propaganda included posters, newspaper advertisements, labels, pamphlets and postcards. All of these ways could spread ideas. If a political message could be passed on in a cartoon, it was often even more popular, so leaders on both sides liked to use cartoons.

Look at these pictures and answer the questions that follow.

a

b

This was produced as a stamp rather than a postcard.

c

d

e

f

Activity

1. Sort the postcards on these two pages into two categories:
   - Unionist
   - Nationalist

2. Look at Source c. What do you notice about the counties named on this postcard? Write two sentences explaining what you have noticed.

3. Compare the pictures of Redmond and Carson (Sources e and f). List the ways in which they are similar.

4. Sources e and f were produced by the same firm. What does this tell us about this firm?

5. Look at Source a. What is the point of view which this postcard is putting forward?

▶

Activity

Divide into groups. Each group should form itself into a 'political' party. Give your party a name. Decide on two main policies. Here are some examples you could use:

- The school needs more litter bins on the campus.
- Anyone who bullies someone should be made to stand in the middle of the car park with a notice saying "I am a bully" tied round their neck.
- Teachers should be appreciated more.
- Cyclists should be banned from major roads.
- Farmers should be allowed to drive tractors on the roads only after six o'clock in the evening.
- School should finish at lunchtime every Friday.
- There should be four school terms in the year instead of three, and the summer holiday should be only four weeks long.
- Dog owners have to buy a dog licence. Cat owners should have to buy a cat licence.

It is coming up to an election and you have to get your policies across to the voters. What do political parties use to spread their policies today?

Plan an election campaign. What media will you use? Who will be your main speakers? Design posters, leaflets etc.

Write a three-minute party political broadcast for television and present it to the class.

Each party should choose three panellists to sit in front of the class and answer questions from the other parties.

At the end, have a secret ballot to vote for the party you think has the best arguments for their policies.

Review this task

Why do you think the winning party was successful?

Of all the methods used to put forward policies, which did you think was most effective?

Which was least effective?

If you were to do this task again, would you do anything differently?

> Design a key fob, a fridge magnet and a car sticker. Make one set for Home Rule supporters and one set for Unionists. Think of snappy slogans which they might have used in 1912.

Research

This is Sir James Craig's house at Craigavon, Co Down, where the 1911 Unionist rally was held. It was built in 1870. The house is still there, off the Outer Ring Road in East Belfast. On the right you can see how it looks now.

> What are the objects on the lawn in the older photograph?
>
> What kind of people do you think lived in this house?
>
> How does the modern picture differ from the older one?

Here is a description of the scene at Craigavon House on 23 September 1911:

"Craigavon was the residence of Captain James Craig, Member of Parliament for East Down. It is a spacious country house standing on a hill above the road leading from Belfast to Holywood, with a fine view of Belfast Lough and the distant Antrim coast beyond the estuary. The lawn in front of the house, sloping steeply to the shore road, forms a sort of natural amphitheatre offering ideal conditions for out-of-door oratory to an unlimited audience. At the meeting on the 23rd of September the platform was erected near the crest of the hill, enabling the vast audience to spread out fan-wise over the lower levels…"

Activity

Prepare a leaflet about Craigavon House, suitable to be given to tourists.

Or

Draw or paint a picture of the mass meeting at Craigavon House in 1911. Use the pictures and description above as a guide.

Rudyard Kipling (1865–1936) was a famous writer. He was born in India when Britain had a great Empire. Kipling supported British rule and was a friend of Edward Carson. He wrote a poem called 'Ulster 1912'. Here are some verses from it.

Rudyard Kipling

Ulster 1912

The dark eleventh hour
Draws on and sees us sold
To every evil power
We fought against of old.
Rebellion, rapine, hate,
Oppression, wrong and greed
Are loosed to rule our fate,
By England's act and deed.

We know the war prepared
On every peaceful home,
We know the hells declared
For such as serve not Rome—
The terror, threats, and dread
In market, hearth, and field—
We know, when all is said,
We perish if we yield.

Believe, we dare not boast,
Believe, we do not fear
We stand to pay the cost
In all that men hold dear.
What answer from the North?
One Law, one Land, one Throne
If England drive us forth
We shall not fall alone!

1. Who is Kipling blaming for what he sees as the threat to the North?

2. What does Kipling mean by the lines: "We know the hells declared/ For such as serve not Rome"?

3. What is his message in the last four lines of the poem?

4. Pick out two lines that you think are the most powerful.

Ulster Day, 28 September 1912

Craig decided to have a **Solemn League and Covenant** for Ulster. The plan was that as many citizens as possible would sign a copy of the Covenant during a week of organised meetings in September 1912. Leading Unionists from England and Ireland would tour Ulster. The week was to end with a huge demonstration in Belfast on Saturday 28 September. This was called **Ulster Day.**

This photograph shows Carson signing the Covenant in Belfast's City Hall. He used a silver pen presented especially for the occasion. The rest of the Unionist leaders signed after him.

Questions

Study the picture of Carson signing the Ulster Covenant. The photograph is old and a little unclear, but can you see Sir James Craig?

1. What is significant about the table?

2. Comment on the group of people around Carson.

3. What is the mood of the occasion?

4. Think of two things that increase the feeling of the importance of the signing.

Ulster's
Solemn League and Covenant.

Being convinced in our consciences that Home Rule would be disastrous to the material well-being of Ulster as well as of the whole of Ireland, subversive of our civil and religious freedom, destructive of our citizenship and perilous to the unity of the Empire, we, whose names are under-written, men of Ulster, loyal subjects of His Gracious Majesty King George V., humbly relying on the God whom our fathers in days of stress and trial confidently trusted, do hereby pledge ourselves in solemn Covenant throughout this our time of threatened calamity to stand by one another in defending for ourselves and our children our cherished position of equal citizen-ship in the United Kingdom and in using all means which may be found necessary to defeat the present conspiracy to set up a Home Rule Parliament in Ireland. ¶ And in the event of such a Parliament being forced upon us we further solemnly and mutually pledge ourselves to refuse to recognise its authority. ¶ In sure confidence that God will defend the right we hereto subscribe our names. ¶ And further, we individually declare that we have not already signed this Covenant.

The above was signed by me at _Mount Joy_

"Ulster Day," Saturday, 28th September, 1912.

David McFarland

——— God Save the King. ———

This is the Covenant which men signed.

This is the version of the Covenant which women signed.

Ulster's
Solemn League and Covenant.

Text of the Covenant made by the Ulster Women's Unionist Council, and which has been signed by the loyal women of Ulster in token of their unwavering hostility to Home Rule:—

WE, whose names are underwritten, women of Ulster, and loyal subjects of our gracious King, being firmly persuaded that Home Rule would be disastrous to our country, desire to associate ourselves with the men of Ulster in their uncompromising opposition to the Home Rule Bill now before Parliament, whereby it is proposed to drive Ulster out of her cherished place in the Constitution of the United Kingdom and to place her under the domination and control of a Parliament in Ireland.

Praying that from this calamity God will save Ireland, we hereto subscribe our names.

The above was signed by me at Omagh
"Ulster Day," Saturday, 28th September, 1912.

God Save the King.

Questions

1. Compare the two versions of the Covenant on these pages. Which one do you think demands most from the person who signs it?
2. What three things did the men agree to?
3. What were the women agreeing to?
4. According to these Covenants, what did the Unionist people fear from an Irish parliament?
5. The Covenant ends with the words "God save the King". Who was the King?
6. Why do you think there were separate Covenants for men and women?

Try this!

The Public Record Office of Northern Ireland (PRONI) holds a huge amount of material. Look up the archives of the Ulster Unionist Council: www.proni.gov.uk/index/search_the_archives/ulster_covenant.htm.

Think of a public figure or a land-owner or even a relative who might have signed the Covenant and look them up on this site. If you click on 'Signature Folder' on the right hand side, you will see a picture of that person's actual signature on a Covenant form.

BY THE WAY

Once the main group had signed, the public were allowed in to the City Hall to sign also. Desks were set out along the corridors for a third of a mile so that 540 signatures could be taken at the same time. So many people had queued that the signing went on until eleven o'clock that night. In total, 237,368 men and 234,046 women signed the covenant. (Source: PRONI) The City Hall in Belfast was opened in 1906, so it was still a new building at this time.
You will find further information at: www.ulstersociety.org/resources/home_rule/ulsterdaybelfast.html

All over Ulster ordinary people signed the Covenant. Some even signed in their own blood! When the figures were added up, over 450,000 men and women had signed the Covenant.

The day was considered a great success. English newspapers told their readers of the great discipline and determination shown by Ulster Unionists during this special week of activity. So the Ulster Covenant not only allowed the Unionist leadership to win back full control of their followers, but it also meant that they got some very good publicity in England.

Activity

1. In your own words, write a paragraph explaining why Carson thought that having an Ulster Day would be a good idea.

2. Write another paragraph explaining what the Unionists felt they gained from the day.

3. Why do you think some men signed the Covenant in their own blood?

Class debate

"In 1912, the Unionists were going against the normal democratic process by refusing to accept the wishes of the majority in Ireland." Discuss this statement.

The Ulster Covenant talked about the nine-county province of Ulster. Because Unionists in Ulster were threatening to use force, another plan was put forward which the government hoped would satisfy them. This was the **county option scheme.** County option meant that any county in Ulster could opt out of a Home Rule parliament for six years. This was to be decided by a vote taken in each county. The likely result of this scheme was that the four counties in North-East Ulster with a Protestant majority – Antrim, Down, Londonderry and Armagh – would opt out of Home Rule.

The idea of special treatment for even four counties of Ulster made Redmond and his fellow Irish Nationalists angry. They made sure that Asquith (the Prime Minister) stuck to the plan of introducing Home Rule for the whole of Ireland.

For the Unionists, on the other hand, the idea of leaving out a certain number of Ulster counties forced them to change their plans. Carson and the other Unionist leaders realised they could not succeed in using Ulster to block Home Rule for the whole of Ireland. The best they could hope for was to keep a number of counties out of the Home Rule plan. The question was, how many counties?

Activity

In groups, write two five-minute speeches, one strongly against allowing any counties to opt out of Home Rule, and the other in favour of allowing it. Carefully argue the case for each opinion.

These maps show the three different options for the area to be left out of Home Rule.

Activity

In groups, prepare arguments in favour of the three alternatives for Northern Ireland in 1914.
4 county
6 county
9 county

Remember (pg 65) when you drew a line on your blank map of Ireland to show where you thought the border should have been drawn? Have you changed your mind about this? Explain your opinion.

Can you draw any conclusions from the fact that, under the county option scheme, counties were to be allowed to opt out of Home Rule for six years?

The Ulster Volunteers

At the end of 1912 the Unionists realised that they would have to step up their resistance if they were going to force Asquith to leave either all or part of Ulster out of the Home Rule Bill. So in January 1913 they formed the **Ulster Volunteer Force (UVF).** The UVF needed 100,000 men and recruiting began immediately. They hadn't very many weapons so the new recruits practised with dummy wooden rifles in Orange Halls all over Ulster.

A group of Ulster Volunteers at Strabane.

Redmond and the Nationalists thought the UVF was a bit of a joke and that they were just bluffing. The government took no action against the UVF even though the Unionists claimed that the UVF would be used against the government if it tried to force Home Rule on Ulster.

The Unionists were determined to make the UVF into a powerful force. To help with training their men, former officers of the British Army were brought in as full-time officers in the UVF. In July 1913 a retired English general, Sir George Richardson, arrived in Belfast to take command of the UVF. Under Richardson's direction, training weekends were held in each county on the estates of rich Unionist landowners. So it was soon clear that the UVF was becoming a well organised, highly trained and very determined force. The only thing missing was weapons, but Unionist leaders had already made secret plans to get weapons.

The Irish Volunteers

Asquith (the Liberal Prime Minister) continued to plan for Home Rule for the whole of Ireland but other members of his government believed that Ulster would have to be treated separately. However, Redmond believed that the Liberal government would go ahead with Home Rule for the whole of Ireland.
Other Nationalists in Ireland believed that the UVF was now so powerful that it could make the Liberal government change its plans. These Nationalists wanted the same kind of force which could make sure that the Liberal government would not give in to the Unionists.

MODERATE: not extreme

So, after seeing how the threat of force had helped the Unionist cause, these Nationalists formed the **Irish Volunteers** in November 1913. Their leader was Eoin MacNeill, one of the founders of the Gaelic League. By the summer of 1914 the Irish Volunteers had well over 100,000 men, making it even bigger than the UVF.

Redmond and the Irish Volunteers

The Irish Volunteers still supported Home Rule, but many of them thought Redmond had become too moderate. More and more people joined the Irish Volunteers. Redmond knew he had to try to get control of it or else he might lose his own place as leader of the Nationalists.
The new force contained members of the old Fenian group which had staged the 1867 Rising. The Fenians were now called the **Irish Republican Brotherhood** (IRB) and many leading IRB figures joined the Irish Volunteers. These men operated secretly within the Irish Volunteers and hoped to use the new force to gain something much more than Home Rule from the British.
They wanted the complete separation of Ireland from Britain, and they were prepared to fight for it.

Activity

This is a group of Irish Volunteers from Co Mayo.

Compare this picture with the picture of Ulster Volunteers on page 80. What similarities and differences do you see?

Two private armies

Asquith was very alarmed that there were now two private armies in Ireland. Both the Ulster Volunteers and the Irish Volunteers wanted to bring weapons into Ireland. Asquith was afraid that this might lead to civil war.

The British government was afraid that the UVF might try to steal weapons from British army stores in Ulster. They thought about sending troops to Ulster from the main Army camp at the Curragh about twenty miles from Dublin. But even before orders to move to the North had been given, more than 50 officers told Army chiefs that they would resign rather than march into Ulster. This became known as **the Curragh Incident** and it put the UVF in a very strong position, because Carson and Craig (who led the UVF) now knew that Asquith couldn't use the British Army against them.

Gun Running at Larne

In April 1914, a large supply of arms was landed in the North. Carson and Craig had given their support to a plan to buy a huge cargo of weapons in Germany and bring them to Ulster. The man in charge of this gun-running plan was Fred Crawford. On the night of the 24/25 April the arms finally arrived in Ulster on board a ship, the *Clyde Valley*.

Most of them were brought to Larne in Co Antrim. That night the UVF blocked off the town of Larne. They had a Motor Car Corps and these cars delivered the rifles all over Ulster very quickly. The police didn't try to stop the unloading and delivery of the weapons. To Nationalists it looked as if the police in Ulster were co-operating with the UVF.

In total nearly 25,000 rifles and three million rounds of ammunition had arrived. Now the Ulster Volunteers had the weapons to back up their threats of resisting Home Rule by force.

TIP

PROJECT

BEFORE YOU START

ACTIVITY

BY THE WAY

SOURCES

WORD BOX

LINK

RESEARCH

Activity

This is a postcard issued in 1914 to show the Larne gun-running.

Study this picture and make a list of everything an historian could gather from it. This postcard was issued by Unionists. Should this affect the way an historian interprets it?

Make a list of all the reasons why, in 1914, Carson, Craig and the UVF had confidence that they would get what they wanted.

Now make a list of all the reasons why they might *not* get what they wanted.

Look at these two lists and say which reasons seem to be the most important in deciding what should happen.

The Howth Gun-running

LIFE-PRESERVER: a long stick that could be used as a weapon.

After the Larne gun-running, the Irish Volunteers were determined to organise their own gun-running. Like the UVF, the Irish Volunteers bought weapons in Germany and then sent them to Ireland on board a yacht. The yacht, the *Asgard*, arrived at Howth, Co Dublin, on 26 July 1914. A total of 1,500 rifles and 45,000 rounds of ammunition were landed at Howth harbour.

Activity

Here is an eyewitness account of landing the guns at Howth. It appeared in the *Irish Times*, 27 July 1914.

"I saw at least a couple of hundred men running for all they were worth towards the pier ... while three or four hundred ran to the head of the pier ... Some of the men were in uniform, some had only badges, but all of them carried long oak life-preservers, and their officers carried revolvers in their hands. The majority of the men seemed to have come from Dublin. While they were running up the pier, the hatches of the yawl [small boat] were opened. Some of the men from the pier jumped down and handed up to their comrades rifles, wrapped in straw ... A very remarkable feature was that the whole affair was conducted almost in silence, very few orders being given."

This is a photograph of the guns being landed at Howth.

Study the eyewitness account and the photograph.

1. Are these primary or secondary sources? Explain your answer.
2. Do you think the eyewitness is (a) sympathetic to the gun-runners (b) hostile to the gun-runners (c) neutral? How can you tell?
3. What could you conclude from the eyewitness's statement: "A very remarkable feature was that the whole affair was conducted almost in silence, very few orders being given."
4. Does the eyewitness account confirm the scene in the photograph?
5. Who do you think might have taken the photograph? Why might they have taken it? Where was the photographer standing? Can you conclude anything from this?

The Batchelor's Walk incident

Unlike Larne, the police at Howth tried to seize the arms that had been unloaded. To do this the police had asked for help and a small number of troops were ordered to the harbour. By this time a crowd had gathered and in the confusion the arms were slipped away in a fleet of taxis that had been waiting near the harbour.

After failing to capture the arms, the soldiers were ordered to march back to Dublin. This was a three-mile march. Some of the crowd followed the soldiers and jeered at them for their failure to seize the arms. When they reached Bachelor's

TIP

PROJECT

BEFORE YOU START

ACTIVITY

BY THE WAY

SOURCES

WORD BOX

LINK

RESEARCH

Walk, which was a quay on the River Liffey, the soldiers suddenly opened fire. Three people were killed and 38 wounded. Nationalists were shocked and furious. They remembered that, only three months earlier, the police had stood by when a much larger shipment of arms had arrived in Larne. It was clear that the Irish Volunteers were being treated very differently to the UVF.

Acitivity

Divide into groups.

You have to put together a report for your local television news about the Bachelor's Walk incident.

Your news editor wants a well-balanced report, giving all the facts and interviews with eyewitnesses, soldiers and members of the crowd.

Imagine you are really there, perhaps an hour after the incident has occurred.

Each member of your group should have a role to play.

Act out your reports for the class.

Draw a picture of the Bachelor's Walk incident. Underneath your picture, in your own words write a short account of what happened. These could be put up on your classroom wall.

Look at each one and point out something that has been done well.

After the Howth gun-running there were two armed camps in Ireland. One in the South was determined to have Home Rule, while the other in the North was equally determined to stop Home Rule.

INEVITABLE: bound to happen; nothing can stop it.

King George V brought the different sides together in July 1914, to try to sort things out, but the talks failed. It seemed as if civil war in Ireland was inevitable.

Do you think the Queen would call a meeting like this today, to discuss a political problem? Why or why not?

But then something happened which drastically affected everything.
While Ireland was preoccupied with its own internal problems, much greater problems were brewing elsewhere.
In August 1914, the **First World War** broke out.
The war with Germany began in August 1914. Both Carson and Redmond wanted to show that their parties would give as much support as possible to Britain.
Despite the war, in September 1914 Asquith decided to sort out the Home Rule mess. Unionists were angry when they learned that Home Rule was going to become law, though it was not to begin until the end of the war.
Asquith had also decided that the question of what to do about Ulster should be put off until the war was over.

LINK TO FIRST WORLD WAR UNIT

You will learn about the Irish in the First World War in the Unit on page 154. Both Carson and Redmond wanted their followers, the Ulster Volunteers and the Irish Volunteers, to join the British Army and help to fight the war against Germany. Apart from the principle of helping to fight against an enemy, each of them thought that, if they gave their support, Britain would find it hard to refuse them what they wanted when the war was over.

Here is a statement from Redmond:

"This war is undertaken in defence of the highest principles of religion and morality and right, and it would be a disgrace forever to our Country… if young Ireland confined her efforts to remaining at home, defending our shore… from unlikely invasion, and shrank from the duty of providing on the field of battle that gallantry and courage which has distinguished our race all through its history."

Activity

Divide into groups.
Pick one person to be a young volunteer in the IVF in 1914. The others in the group are his or her friends. You are all on Twitter. The volunteer has to decide whether to do as Redmond wishes and join the British Army. On a file pad, write out an exchange of comments between friends on Twitter. The volunteer is putting forward his or her own thoughts in short messages and friends are responding with their own short comments and giving their views on what to do. You have only 140 characters, including spaces, for each comment. There should be a wide range of views represented.
When you have finished, each group should read out their Twitter exchange and each volunteer should say what he or she has decided to do.

Carson at a UVF rally.

Sir Edward Carson told the government that the members of the Ulster Volunteers would be ready and willing to serve in the British Army. The UVF were given their own special division in the army, the **36th Ulster Division.** Carson, Craig and the other Unionist leaders encouraged their supporters to join the new Ulster Division.
Carson said, "All officers, non-commissioned officers and men who are in the Ulster Volunteer Force… are requested to answer immediately His Majesty's call, as our first duty as loyal subjects is to the King…"

TIP

PROJECT

BEFORE YOU
START

ACTIVITY

BY THE WAY

SOURCES

WORD BOX

LINK

RESEARCH

The *Belfast Newsletter* reported that 35,000 men from Ulster had joined the British Army.

Here is what the *Belfast Newsletter* reported in August 1914:

> The organisation [UVF] has risen to a great occasion with ... enthusiasm ... bearing out to the full the frequent references of Sir Edward Carson to the loyalty of the Force and their readiness to do everything in their power to uphold [Britain] and to maintain the honour and prestige of the Empire.

BY THE WAY

The *Belfast Newsletter* is the oldest newspaper in the world to have been in continuous production since it was founded in 1737. It was founded by Francis Joy who acquired a printing press as a settlement of a debt. It was first printed in Joy's Entry in Belfast.

Activity

You have listened to what Carson said. Write an e-mail to a friend, explaining in your own words what Carson's argument is.

Tell your friend what *your* opinion is on what he said.

Send your email.

Read the newspaper clipping below and answer the question that follows.
The Royal Inniskillings were a British Army regiment.

The *Irish News* published the following in August 1914:

TYRONE'S FINE EXAMPLE.

NATIONAL AND ULSTER VOLUNTEERS MARCH TOGETHER.
ROUSING SCENES

The Ulster Volunteers and Irish National Volunteers united at Omagh on Friday night in giving a most hearty send-off to the final draft of the Army Reserve of the Royal Inniskillings, who left the town about half-past nine o'clock, and a scene of an unparalleled description was witnessed when the procession of both bodies of Volunteers and military marched through the town together…Subsequently, as both bodies of Volunteers paraded the town, they met one another and respectfully saluted.

The Ulster Volunteers and Irish Volunteers respected each other on this occasion. What was it about the occasion that made this happen?

The war caused a very significant split in the Irish Volunteers. The majority agreed with Redmond and joined the British Army. A minority, about 10,000, disagreed and broke away. They kept the name 'Irish Volunteers' and Redmond's followers became known as the '**National Volunteers**'.

Activity

Study this cartoon. You will find another picture on page 171 interesting to compare with this one.
Discuss the cartoon.
Who are the skeletons?
Who is the man in the picture at the top of the cartoon?
What country is this scene in?
Which flag is shown on the hill and why?
Who do you think the artist supports?
What is the message of this cartoon?

This is a long Unit and we'll stop for a breather here! In the next Unit, we'll consider what happened in Ireland during the First World War and the years that followed.

Your Timeline
Draw a timeline and mark on it all the dates that you have read about in this chapter and what happened on those dates.

Activity

Look at your timeline and pick out one person or event that you would like to know more about.

Investigate this person or event and then decide on the best way to present your findings. This might be the way you feel most confident with, or you might find, for example, that you have found a lot of illustrations and you would like to show them in a PowerPoint presentation.

Consider these methods:

> A short booklet or leaflet
> A folder of information
> A PowerPoint presentation
> A wall display
> A short talk to the class
> A roll-play of the event (team up with a partner if necessary)
> A blog entry

When you have finished, discuss your work with your teacher and explain why you chose that method of presentation.

Activity

Pick one event from this Unit and write a fictional story about someone who was there at the time.

Your main character could be yourself or someone else. If the main character is yourself, then write the story in the *first person.* This means that you say things like: "*I* saw…", "*I* said…".

If the main character is someone else, you write your story in the *third person*. This means that you say things like: "*He* saw…" or "*She* said…".

FICTIONAL: made up, didn't really happen.

Swop stories with a partner and tell them two things you liked about their story. Is there one thing that you think could have been done better?

Class Quiz!

Divide into two teams and decide on a prize for the winning team. If you get a question right, your team gets a point, BUT if you get a question wrong, you lose a point!

1. What was the name of Sir James Craig's house?
2. Into what port did the Irish Volunteers smuggle guns?
3. Name the river that flows through Dublin.
4. Name the nine counties of Ulster.
5. Which counties were suggested for the option of a four-county Northern Ireland?
6. Who wrote the poem 'Ulster 1912'?
7. By what name was 28 September, 1912, known?
8. Who was the British Prime Minister who introduced the Third Home Rule Bill?
9. The Ulster Volunteers smuggled guns into Portrush. True or false?
10. Who was the leader of the Irish Nationalists in 1912?
11. Name the three countries to which most Irish emigrants went.
12. What office did the representative of the sovereign in Ireland hold at the beginning of the twentieth century?
13. Who was the founder of Sinn Féin?
14. Where did Edward Carson sign the Ulster Covenant?
15. What was the approximate population of Ireland in 1901?
16. With what did Edward Carson sign the Ulster Covenant?
17. Who was the leader of the Irish Volunteers?
18. What was the Curragh Incident?
19. What was the name of the boat which brought in the guns for the Irish Volunteers?
20. What happened in 1914 to postpone the Home Rule issue?

Word Check

Check out these words to make sure you can spell them.

Howth	economically	residence
emigration	foreign	Craig
separate	opposition	sectarian
settlement	business	solemn
population	Asquith	ammunition
Gaelic	appreciate	pier
celebration	persuasion	

If you're not sure if you can spell any of them, check them out a few more times.

Review this Unit

Look over this Unit again and make sure that you understand all that happened.
Discuss with your teacher any sections that you found difficult.
Has anything that you learned in this Unit come as a surprise to you?

TIP

PROJECT

BEFORE YOU START

ACTIVITY

BY THE WAY

SOURCES

WORD BOX

LINK

RESEARCH

IRELAND
FROM THE OUTBREAK OF WAR IN 1914

Alice Milligan (1866–1953, pictured right) was an Irish nationalist, a Protestant, writer and lecturer for the Gaelic League. She was fiercely dedicated to Ireland and antagonistic to British rule. In the late 1890s, she wrote a column for a newspaper in which she said:

"... all my own aspirations come, not from those who are busy in the living world, so much as from the dead. It is they above all whose wishes, when we remember them, are commands we dare not shrink from obeying, whose unfulfilled hopes we treasure tenderly."

Discuss what Alice Milligan said.

What do you think she meant?

Do you agree with her?

Many events in history are remembered and even celebrated today. Is it always right to do so?

BEFORE YOU START

You remember that, in 1914, John Redmond had asked the Irish Volunteers to enlist in the British Army to fight in the First World War. A number of members had so strongly disagreed with this that they broke away. This group kept the name Irish Volunteers. Redmond's supporters, by far the majority, took the name National Volunteers.

When the First World War started, most people thought that it would last only a few months. But as time went on it seemed more likely that it could last for years. Irishmen who had originally supported Redmond in his wartime support for Britain, now began to turn against him.

The breakaway group of Irish Volunteers under Eoin MacNeill was still training. This group of Irish Volunteers included a number of revolutionary nationalists or republicans who were members of the secret IRB (Irish Republican Brotherhood). Some of these IRB men began to plan a rising (rebellion) in which they hoped to use the Irish Volunteers to drive the British out of Ireland. This was going much further than Home Rule. They wanted total independence from Britain.

Patrick Pearse

The main person planning the Rising was a Dublin teacher called Patrick Pearse. Pearse had been an enthusiastic member of the Gaelic League. In 1908 he started a school, St Enda's, which had all of its subjects taught in Irish. Others involved in the planning of a rising had also become interested in politics by being members of the Gaelic League.

Patrick Pearse was a great speaker. When a founder member of the Irish Republican Brotherhood, O'Donovan Rossa, died in 1915, Pearse gave the oration at the huge funeral in Glasnevein

BY THE WAY

St Enda's School in Rathfarnam, Dublin, is now the Pearse Museum, dedicated to illustrating his life and achievements. Rathfarnam gets its name from the Irish, Rath Fearnain (pronounced 'rath farnan') which means 'Fearnain's ringfort'.

LINK TO IRELAND 2 UNIT

ORATION: a formal public speech at a special occasion, specially a funeral.

Cemetery in Dublin. This was one of the most influential speeches ever given in Ireland. He finished it with the words:

"Life springs from death; and from the graves of patriot men and women spring living nations. The Defenders of this Realm have worked well in secret and in the open. They [the British] think that they have pacified Ireland. They think that they have purchased half of us and intimidated the other half. They think that they have foreseen everything, think that they have provided against everything; but the fools, the fools, the fools! — they have left us our Fenian dead, and while Ireland holds these graves, Ireland unfree shall never be at peace."

Questions

Discuss the extract above from Pearse's oration.

1. Who is Pearse's audience and what opinions are they likely to hold?

2. Do you see any similarities with the sentiments expressed by Alice Milligan in the extract at the beginning of this Unit? If so, what are they?

3. What was Pearse referring to when he said: "They think that they have pacified Ireland. They think that they have purchased half of us and intimidated the other half."?

4. What do you see in this extract which makes it a good speech? What speaking techniques does Pearse use?

5. What can a speaker add to his message that a writer cannot?

Activity

Now it's your turn!

Write a five-minute speech about something you feel strongly.

- Write out your headings and arrange them in the order in which you want to talk about them.

- Write a careful introduction. This should catch the attention of your audience and keep them listening.

- Write the main body of your speech, following the order you decided on. Use persuasive language and memorable phrases. Remember, you will be *speaking* this.

- Write your conclusion. This should sum up your arguments and inspire your audience to agree with you.

The next stage is very important! Read your speech to yourself. Hear it in your own head. Does it sound right? Is it the best you can achieve? Could you change a word or a phrase to a stronger one? Would, for example, your second point be better swopped with your third point?

Once you have checked it over, rehearse it again thinking of what tone of voice and volume you should use for different parts of your speech. Time yourself. If you

TIP

PROJECT

BEFORE YOU START

ACTIVITY

BY THE WAY

SOURCES

WORD BOX

LINK
RESEARCH

are asked to give a speech, you need to know how long you have been given to speak. Is your speech long enough or is it too long?

Now you are ready to give your speech to the class if your teacher picks you.

....

There was a slogan used by the Fenians in the previous century:

ENGLAND'S DIFFICULTY IS IRELAND'S OPPORTUNITY

It was used again in the events leading up to the Easter Rising. What do you think this slogan meant?

....

The date of the Rising was fixed for Easter 1916. Even though it was possible that they would die, the rebels thought of their deaths as being the blood sacrifice that they had spoken of before. Their deaths would make everyone demand freedom from British rule in Ireland.

The Rising began on Easter Monday, 24 April 1916. The rebels took over a number of important buildings in Dublin, such as the Jacob's Factory and Boland's Mills. The Volunteers' headquarters was the General Post Office (GPO) in O'Connell Street. They flew the flag of the Irish Republic over the building, and Pearse stood outside to read the Proclamation of the Republic. You can read the text of the Proclamation on the next page. Normal life was going on in the city and the small crowd which gathered to listen to Pearse was amazed at what was going on. The Rising was a surprise to most people in Britain and Ireland.

The Irish Volunteers waited in the buildings until they were attacked. It wasn't long before they knew they were defeated.

POBLACHT NA H EIREANN
THE PROVISIONAL GOVERNMENT
OF THE
IRISH REPUBLIC
TO THE PEOPLE OF IRELAND

POBLACHT NA H EIREANN

THE PROVISIONAL GOVERNMENT

OF THE

IRISH REPUBLIC

TO THE PEOPLE OF IRELAND

IRISHMEN AND IRISHWOMEN: In the name of God and of the dead generations from which she receives her old tradition of nationhood, Ireland, through us, summons her children to her flag and strikes for her freedom.

Having organised and trained her manhood through her secret revolutionary organisation, the Irish Republican Brotherhood, and through her open military organisations, the Irish Volunteers and the Irish Citizen Army, having patiently perfected her discipline, having resolutely waited for the right moment to reveal itself, she now seizes that moment, and, supported by her exiled children in America and by gallant allies in Europe, but relying in the first on her own strength, she strikes in full confidence of victory.

We declare the right of the people of Ireland to the ownership of Ireland, and to the unfettered control of Irish destinies, to be sovereign and indefeasible. The long usurpation of that right by a foreign people and government has not extinguished the right, nor can it ever be extinguished except by the destruction of the Irish people. In every generation the Irish people have asserted their right to national freedom and sovereignty: six times during the past three hundred years they have asserted it in arms. Standing on that fundamental right and again asserting it in arms in the face of the world, we hereby proclaim the Irish Republic as a Sovereign Independent State, and we pledge our lives and the lives of our comrades-in-arms to the cause of its freedom, of its welfare, and its exaltation among the nations.

The Irish Republic is entitled to, and hereby claims, the allegiance of every Irishman and Irishwoman. The Republic guarantees religious and civil liberty, equal rights and equal opportunities to all its citizens, and declares its resolve to pursue the happiness and prosperity of the whole nation and of all its parts, cherishing all the children of the nation equally, and oblivious of the differences carefully fostered by an alien government, which have divided a minority from the majority in the past.

Until our arms have brought the opportune moment for the establishment of a permanent National Government, representative of the whole people of Ireland and elected by the suffrages of all her men and women, the Provisional Government, hereby constituted, will administer the civil and military affairs of the Republic in trust for the people.

We place the cause of the Irish Republic under the protection of the Most High God, Whose blessing we invoke upon our arms, and we pray that no one who serves that cause will dishonour it by cowardice, inhumanity, or rapine. In this supreme hour the Irish nation must, by its valour and discipline and by the readiness of its children to sacrifice themselves for the common good, prove itself worthy of the august destiny to which it is called.

TIP

PROJECT

BEFORE YOU START

ACTIVITY

BY THE WAY

SOURCES

WORD BOX

LINK

RESEARCH

Questions

Study the Proclamation and discuss the following questions.

1. How would you describe the overall tone of the Proclamation?
   Pick out words and sentences which give you this impression.

2. The second last paragraph states that the National Government shall be: "representative of the whole people of Ireland and elected by the suffrages of all her men and women".

   What can you conclude about the views of the writers of the Proclamation on:

   (a) what land constituted the Irish Republic?

   (b) who should be able to vote in elections?

Activity

Here is an artist's impression of the scene inside the General Post Office, Dublin, just before the surrender, Easter, 1916. Pearse (ringed) stands, bare-headed and holding a revolver. Study the picture carefully.

1. What words would you use to describe this scene?

2. Is fighting still going on? How do you know?

3. How reliable do you think this picture is as a record of the scene inside the GPO?

The rebels' position was hopeless. On Saturday 29 April, Pearse surrendered. The fighting had lasted less than a week and about 450 people were killed. Most people in Dublin were very angry with the Easter rebels and blamed them for the terrible damage which had been done to the city during the fighting.

TIP

You should find that the tricolour is not the first flag used by Irish rebels against English rule, but you will have to go back to the eighteenth century to find out more about that. 'Tricolour' means 'three-colour'.

Project

Here is a photograph of the GPO in O'Connell Street, Dublin, as it looks today. You can see the flag of the Republic of Ireland flying over it. The rebels flew a similar one at Easter, 1916. Your task is to find out the history of the Irish flag.

Word process your findings in a carefully formatted document. Use illustrations if you can.

This is a photograph of the centre of Dublin after the Rising. O'Connell Street is in the foreground and the River Liffey is on the right.

Activity

This is a photograph taken inside the GPO after the Rising was over.

1. How do you think the damage you can see was caused?

2. Who are the people in uniform?

3. What kind of smell would be in the GPO when this photograph was taken?

4. Compare this photograph with the painting on page 95. Can you see anything that is the same in both pictures?

5. As you can see from the photograph of the GPO today, it is an impressive building. How would an ordinary person in Dublin have felt about the damage caused to it?

Executions

After the Rising, the British decided that the rebels should be severely punished. They were kept in Kilmainham Gaol in Dublin, where fifteen of the leaders were executed by firing squad between the 3 and 12 of May. By the time the last leader, **James Connolly**, was executed most people were sympathetic to the Easter rebels. Connolly had been wounded during the fighting. You can see him on the stretcher in the painting on page 95. He was unable to stand up so he was tied to a chair to face the firing squad.

In fact, the way Connolly was executed made many Irish people think of the leaders of the Easter Rising as heroes.

Many of those who were interned or imprisoned without trial were members of Sinn Féin though they may not have taken part in the Rising. The Government wrongly believed that Sinn Féin had organised the Rising and continued to arrest members throughout 1917.

When the First World War ended in December 1918, the Government held a General Election. Out of 105 seats in Ireland, 73 were taken by Sinn Féin. Those elected included Countess Markievicz – the first woman to be elected to the House of Commons. The Unionist party held 26 seats and the Home Rule group held 6.

Activity

Look at the two block diagrams of election results in Ireland in 1910 and 1918 Explain why the votes for Sinn Féin increased between 1910 and 1918.

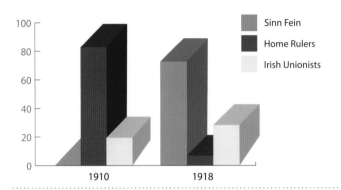

Sinn Féin MP's refused to go to Westminster to take their seats. Instead, they formed their own parliament in Dublin – **Dáil Eireann**. A Prime Minister was appointed; he was to be called the **Taoiseach**. On 29 January 1919 they declared Ireland to be an independent republic and **Eamon de Valera** was confirmed as President.

Activity

Results of the Rising

Read the following statements and say which are:

(a) long term results of the Rising

(b) short term results of the Rising

(c) immediate results of the Rising

1. 2,500 people were wounded

2. In 1917 a republican Thomas Ashe died on hunger strike. Tens of thousands attended his funeral.

3. There were many raids on the houses of ordinary people, especially in Dublin right through the summer months.

4. The Unionists were even more determined to have nothing to do with Dublin.

5. The centre of Dublin was destroyed.

6. There was a General Election in 1918 and Sinn Féin won over 70 seats while the Home Rule Party won 6.

7. People began to take an interest in Pearse and his friends.

TIP

PROJECT

BEFORE YOU
START

ACTIVITY

BY THE WAY

SOURCES

WORD BOX

LINK

RESEARCH

8. People who worked in the city centre lost their jobs.

9. Innocent and angry young men in prison camps were ready to listen to IRB members.

10. 450+ people had died including about 300 civilians.

11. When people heard about the executions and prison camps they gradually began to change their minds about the rebels.

12. £2,500,000 worth of damage was done to the city.

13. Between 3 and 12 May, 15 of the leaders were secretly tried and executed.

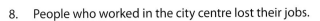

Activity

This is a photograph of the first Dáil Eireann. It was taken on 10 April 1919.

Eamon de Valera is in the centre of the front row and Arthur Griffith is to *de Valera's right*. Is he the man with the walking stick or the man with the white beard?

Discuss this photograph in class. For example, what do you notice about the ages of the people? From this, what can you conclude about the experiences and past history of some of the members?

What else do you notice?

The War of Independence

Black and Tans on guard duty in Dublin in 1920.

Britain refused to accept this declaration of independence and didn't recognise the Dáil.

Violence started up again. The Irish Republican Army fought for the new republic. They were led by **Michael Collins.** They used guerrilla warfare, mainly attacks on police and army forces. The first incident was at Soloheadbeg in County Tipperary. There was an attack on police and two Royal Irish Constabulary officers were killed.

The British Prime Minister, Lloyd George, sent reinforcements to help the police. They were mainly unemployed ex-servicemen. They wore a makeshift uniform, a mixture of police black and army khaki. Because of this uniform, they were called the **Black and Tans.**

The Black and Tans soon got a reputation for brutality. If they were attacked they quickly took revenge. They burnt houses and shot suspects and caused many to support the nationalists.

COM
TPD
BC

GUERRILLA WARFARE: a type of fighting where the fighters don't openly face their enemy in battle but make surprise raids and generally harass the opposing force.

Activity

Here is what one man, Danny, remembered of the Black and Tans in Cork City about 1920. He was just a child of ten years old at the time.

"Me and my friend Jimmy were just running about on the street playing one day and these Black and Tans came along in an armoured car. They stopped and got out and searched us. They found a wee green and gold ribbon in Jimmy's pocket. They got him into the armoured car and drove him miles out into the country and dumped him. He had to walk all the way home. He was really scared. I ran home to tell my mum. She was furious. Jimmy was from an ordinary law-abiding family. Protestants in fact, not like us. They'd never had a bit of trouble before."

1. Why did the Black and Tans find the green and gold ribbon significant?

2. How do you think Jimmy's family felt after this incident?

3. Danny's mum phones Jimmy's mum to talk over the incident. Role-play the conversation that they have. What are they likely to say to each other? Will their attitudes to the incident be (i) the same, (ii) slightly different or (iii) very different?

Even though there was great violence during the War of Independence, support for Sinn Féin stayed strong and demands increased for the British to find a peaceful solution. Negotiations had been taking place to solve the problem of the Unionists.

It was decided to divide the island of Ireland into two sections. The province of Ulster was to be called Northern Ireland but at the last minute the number of counties to be included was reduced from nine to six. The Unionists were happy with this as six counties gave a safer majority to Unionists who would have been weaker in a nine county state. Can you remember why?

The partition of Ireland came into force through the Government Of Ireland Act 1920

Northern Ireland .... 6 counties
Southern Ireland .... 26 counties

A parliament would be set up in Belfast to administer Northern Ireland

A parliament would be set up in Dublin to administer Southern Ireland

In effect both groups were given Home Rule.

Partition was not to be permanent – a Council of Ireland was set up and each country would send representatives who would merge the two states when they felt the time was right.

Both parliaments were to send MPs to Westminster.

Northern Ireland accepted this Act.

Southern Ireland didn't accept the Act and fighting continued. However, an election was held for the Southern Parliament and those elected went to the Dáil instead.

The first Parliament of Northern Ireland was held in Belfast City Hall in 1921 and was opened by King George V. The Parliament normally met in the Presbyterian Church's Assemblies' Buildings in Botanic Avenue in Belfast, although the official opening by the King was held in the City Hall.

The official opening of the Northern Ireland parliament in 1921.

Look at this picture. It was taken in 1921, between Newry and Dundalk, just south of the new border.

These carriages were blown up by the IRA. Can you see horses lying dead and injured? The train was transporting horses from the official parade that accompanied King George V and Queen Mary to the official opening of the Northern Ireland Parliament. The horses were on their way to Dublin to be taken back on the ferry to Holyhead in Wales. Four people and 80 horses were killed. Why do you think the IRA blew up this train?
Do you think all nationalists would have supported this attack?

Parliament Buildings at Stormont were a gift from the British Government and were completed in 1932.

Research

In groups, research the history of Parliament Buildings at Stormont.

You must find out:

- where it is
- when work was started and how long it took to build
- in what architectural style it is finished
- with what stone it is built
- who laid the foundation stone and on what date
- who performed the opening ceremony and one interesting fact about this person
- in what townland it is
- what was done to the building during the Second World War and why

As part of your research, make a note of all the sources you used to find your information. All good research includes these references in case you, or someone else, wants to look up something again.

Activity

Use the picture opposite, or another picture you might find on the Internet, to draw your own picture of Parliament Buildings at Stormont.

BY THE WAY

Ireland has a unique system of land division. The whole island of Ireland is divided into townlands. There are about 64,000 of them! The townland name is used in addresses in the Republic of Ireland. In Northern Ireland in the 1970s, the Post Office decided to give every road a name and every house on the road a number, even farms and cottages in the middle of the countryside. This was a very controversial decision and in 2001 the Northern Ireland Assembly passed a motion requesting government departments to make use of townland addresses in correspondence and publications. Townlands are important still because, for example, they are often used in legal documents to describe what land a person owns. They are also very useful for tracing the history of a place or family ancestry.

Some local councils put the road and townland name together on signs. See if you can spot any signs like these. Do you know what townland you live in? If not, do some research on the Internet to find out.

Although the Nationalists didn't like the terms of the Government of Ireland Act, they realised they wouldn't be able to get Britain out of Ireland completely. A Truce was agreed in July 1921, and President de Valera sent an Irish delegation to London to talk to Lloyd George. The two men who went were Michael Collins and Arthur Griffith.

They did reach an agreement. This was the **Anglo-Irish Treaty**, agreed in December 1921.

- The British recognised the Dáil as the parliament of the twenty-six counties.
- Ireland would be independent of Britain but would stay in the British Empire.
- All members of the Dáil would have to swear allegiance to the British King or Queen.
- Collins and Griffith also agreed to cooperate with Britain if any wars broke out.
- As part of this, the Irish allowed Britain to keep control of three ports from which they could operate British ships. These were called the **Treaty Ports** and were at Berehaven, Queenstown (modern Cobh) and Lough Swilly.

> **DELEGATION:** a small number of people sent to represent a larger group.

Map of Ireland showing the Treaty Ports.

Activity

Look at the map showing the three Treaty Ports.

Why do you think Britain wanted to keep these ports? Think about where they are and what sort of ships are able to enter them.

BY THE WAY

These ports remained under the control of the UK until 1938, when they were returned to Ireland. From an Irish point of view, the handing back of the ports coming up to the Second World War was important because Ireland had decided to be neutral in the war.

Britain agreed to set up a **Boundary Commission** to look at where the border had been drawn. The Irish delegation thought that this Commission would recommend redrawing the border so that Counties Fermanagh and Tyrone, South Down, South Armagh and most of Derry would be removed from Northern Ireland. This would leave Northern Ireland very small indeed and it wouldn't be able to survive as a state.

Activity

Read through the terms of the **Anglo-Irish Treaty.**
Which terms would have pleased the Irish?
Which terms would have pleased the British?

Michael Collins believed there was no choice except to sign this Treaty.
He wrote a letter on the night it was signed.

> 2:00 am December 6th, 1921
>
> Think what I have got for Ireland? Something she has wanted these past 700 years. Will anyone be satisfied at the bargain? Will anyone? I tell you, early this morning I signed my death warrant.

Question

Why do you think Collins felt that he had signed his death warrant?

The Anglo-Irish Treaty caused a bitter split in nationalism in Ireland. Those who opposed the Treaty felt that they had been betrayed, both by the agreement to allow Britain to keep three Irish ports and because complete independence from Britain had not been achieved,

Eamon de Valera didn't accept the Treaty and formed his own force to fight against those who accepted it. He said:

"I am … asking you to reject the Treaty for two reasons … it gives away Irish independence, it brings us into the British Empire, it acknowledges the head of the British Empire … as the direct monarch of Ireland [and] as the source of … authority in Ireland.'

Arthur Griffith agreed with the Treaty. He said:

"It is the first Treaty that admits the equality of Ireland … we have brought back the evacuation of Ireland after 700 years by British troops."

Another member of the Irish Parliament said:

"I am opposed to the Treaty because it gives away our allegiance and perpetuates partition … When did the achievement of our nation's unification cease to be one of our national aspirations?"

A vote on whether to accept the Treaty or not was taken in the Dáil in January 1922. The result was:

For----------------64

Against---------- 57

Activity

To the nearest per cent, what percentage of those who voted, voted *against* the Treaty?

....

De Valera resigned and Arthur Griffith became President of Dáil Eireann.

A **civil war** began in Ireland. De Valera's forces fought against the army of the new **Free State**, as it was called. As he had predicted, Michael Collins was ambushed near his home in west Cork and shot dead.

The Civil War was particularly violent and ruthless. Many of those who suffered during it remained very bitter for the rest of their lives. Unlike fighting the British, the 'struggle' had turned into Irishmen fighting Irishmen. More people were killed during the Civil War than during the War of Independence.

TIP

PROJECT

BEFORE YOU START

ACTIVITY

BY THE WAY

SOURCES

WORD BOX

LINK

RESEARCH

Activity

Discuss the effects of a civil war on a society.

Think of all the things that can happen.

How might it make people feel about each other?

For how long can the consequences of a civil war be felt?

By 1923 de Valera realised he couldn't win and called a ceasefire. The army of the new state had won.
De Valera formed a new political party which came to be called **Fianna Fáil**.
The party of those who had supported the Treaty came to be known as **Fine Gael**.
These are still the main parties in the Dáil today.

Activity

Divide into groups and discuss the following questions.

1. Has your study of the causes of the partition of Ireland made you change your view of how you see the situation in Ireland today?

2. Do *you* think that dividing the island was the best solution for the situation? Give reasons for your opinions.

3. Can you think of any other ways in which the situation could have been handled?

So how were the six northern counties affected by partition?

The Civil War of 1922–23 preoccupied Irish forces during a critical time in the establishment of the Northern Ireland state. This meant that Northern Ireland was forgotten about as an issue for several years. So a civil war between unionists in the north and nationalists in the south didn't happen. Also, Northern Ireland was mostly unaffected by the Civil War in the rest of the country.

Sir James Craig became the first Prime Minister of Northern Ireland.

The Six Counties, as they are sometimes called, remained confident in their Protestant origins, just as the twenty-six counties were proud of their Catholic foundation.

Activity

Look at the following quotations and answer the questions which follow.

 Éamon de Valera: "Since the coming of St Patrick 1500 years ago Ireland has been a Christian and a Catholic nation ... she will remain a Catholic nation." (March 1935)

 Sir James Craig: "All I boast is that we are a Protestant Parliament and Protestant State." (24 April 1934)

 Éamon de Valera: "I say the people of Mayo, in a county where I think 98% of the population is Catholic, are justified in insisting on a Catholic librarian." (June 1930. A well qualified librarian had been sacked because she was a Protestant.)

 The wife of Terence O'Neill, Prime Minister of Northern Ireland, 1963–69, advertising in the *Belfast Telegraph*: "Protestant girl required for housework."

 Éamon de Valera: "A Protestant doctor ought not to be appointed as a dispensary doctor in a mainly Catholic area." (June 1930)

 Terence O'Neill: "It is frightfully hard to explain to Protestants that if you give Roman Catholics a good job and a good house, they will live like Protestants because they will see neighbours with cars and television sets; they will refuse to have eighteen children ... If you treat Roman Catholics with due consideration and kindness, they will live like Protestants in spite of the authoritative nature of their Church ..." (Interview with the *Belfast Telegraph*, 10 May 1969.)

1. If these quotations were the only sources you had, which state would you judge to be the most sectarian?

2. Do you think any of these statements would be acceptable now? Why or why not?

TIP

PROJECT

BEFORE YOU START

ACTIVITY

BY THE WAY

SOURCES

WORD BOX

LINK

RESEARCH

Activity

You remember that there are nine counties in Ulster.

Name them all again. Which three counties were left out of the new northern state after Ireland was partitioned?

There were unionists in these three counties who had been enthusiastic supporters of Carson and Craig in their resistance to Home Rule. In fact there had been major rallies in these counties to which Carson had come to speak.

Read the following extract:

"... to the horror of Donegal's Unionists, Carson and the other northerners accepted [a six county state]. ... it became completely clear to the county's loyalists that the promises had been empty and that the unionists of the rest of Ulster were content to win a parliament for themselves and leave Donegal to fend for itself."

From www.askaboutireland.ie *accessed 27/8/09*

It is 1920. The decision to include only six counties in the new state has just been made. A television station has come to talk to a unionist farmer living in Co Monaghan. What questions will the interviewer ask and what is the farmer likely to say? Remember a recent world event as well as the partition issue.

Role-play the interview.

The new border gave rise to some awkward situations. In some places it ran through the middle of farms and split the farmer's land in two. He might live in the north and have cattle in fields in the south!

Because the two parts of the country became economically separate, there had to be customs posts along the border. Local people smuggled goods into the south if they were cheaper in the north. As well as main roads, there were lots of small country roads that crossed over where the border had been drawn. After Partition, these roads were sometimes blocked or marked with a sign 'Unapproved Road'.

Here is what one man remembered, when he was a boy of ten living in Monaghan.

"My dad and a few others used to drive six-and-a-half miles into South Armagh, down a wee unapproved road to a grocery shop run by friends of ours. They had got caught on the north side. My dad would buy a whole box of butter and nip back across the border again."

A woman from Cavan recalled: "We weren't very political at all, just moderate nationalists and we really resented the border. We had never asked for it. They just stuck it there, and cut us off from lots of places we were used to going and friends we couldn't visit without going through this whole customs procedure."

Activity

Draw two columns in your notebook. Call one column 'Nationalists' and the other column 'Unionists'. In each column list reasons why each of these groups of people living near the new border would *not* have liked it.

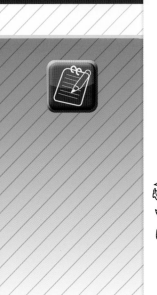

"On the other hand, it's quite possible his story of taking a wrong turning could be perfectly true."

Activity

Study this cartoon.

The caption reads "On the other hand, it's quite possible his story of taking a wrong turning could be perfectly true."

What situation is the cartoonist portraying?

What do you think is the cartoonist's opinion of the situation?

Donegal and Derry were particularly affected by Partition. Look at this map.

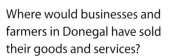

Where do you think customers and clients for businesses in Derry would have come from?

Where would businesses and farmers in Donegal have sold their goods and services?

Railways were badly affected by Partition. Because of the way the border was drawn, the railway between Clones in Co Monaghan and Cavan town – both in the south – crossed the border into Northern Ireland several times! Look at the large scale inset to see why. The train didn't stop because there were no stations on the northern sections so no-one got on or off in the North.

In 1913, a new railway was opened between Armagh and Castleblaney, going via Keady. The main purpose of this new railway was to help farmers going to Castleblaney fair from Keady and other parts of South Armagh, to sell livestock. Because of the border, it was no longer viable to take livestock to Castleblaney because of the customs regulations. So the main purpose of the line had been taken away and the railway closed to passengers in 1923.

The Second World War broke out in 1939. The south of Ireland was neutral, but Northern Ireland was still in the United Kingdom and it was at war with Germany. At first, many people thought that Northern Ireland was too far away from Germany to be affected very much. However, in April and May 1941, German bombers raided Belfast four times. This became known as the **Belfast Blitz** and 955 people were killed.

In April 1941, two bombs were dropped on Derry and thirteen people were killed.

VIABLE: workable

Activity

Study the table below.
Belfast suffered only four air raids but more people were killed in them than in Southampton and Portsmouth. Give reasons that could account for this.

City	Raids	Killed	Injured	Houses damaged or destroyed
Belfast	4	955	2436	56,885
Coventry	43	1251	1859	54,373
Hull	82	c1200	c1800	86,722
Southampton	57	633	1908	43,289
Portmouth	67	930	2837	13,174

Part of the Antrim Road in Belfast after a German air raid, 15/16 April 1941.

Questions

1. Why do you think someone took this picture?

2. Photographers often record scenes in war time, often risking their own lives to do so. What are the advantages of these photographs to an historian?

**LINK TO
MEDICINE UNIT**

When the United States of America entered the war in 1941, American airmen were sent to bases in Northern Ireland. Many of these men married girls they met in Northern Ireland and they went back to America with their new husbands. These girls were called '**GI Brides**'. (GI is a nickname for an American soldier.) There are lots of reasons why so many Americans can trace their family roots back to Ireland – this is one of them!

When the Welfare State was introduced in 1948, people in Northern Ireland were able to benefit from it. The standard of living rose for many poorer people, an advantage which those in the south didn't have.

One woman recalled an incident when she fell through the glass of her father's greenhouse in Co Donegal when she was a small child.

"A piece of glass split my cheek open and I nearly lost my eye. My parents rushed me to a doctor in Donegal town and he sewed the edges of the cut together with four big stitches while I sat on my father's knee. But it wasn't done right and left quite an ugly scar on my face. When my parents moved to the North because of my father's job, they took me to a hospital in Belfast and the doctors there brought me into hospital and opened up the scar and stitched it up again with tiny stitches. You wouldn't see the scar now unless you really looked closely. If we'd stayed in the south, my parents couldn't have afforded to get that sort of treatment for me. As it turned out, they didn't have to pay a thing."

The main legacy of the partition of Ireland is the continuing discontent of those people whose families never wanted it to happen and feel that the border should be abolished, or those whose families want to make sure the six northern counties remain under British rule. Although there are very few people still alive who lived through the War of Independence, the Civil War and Partition, the memory of those days is still very strong today.

This has led to trouble and much violence and over 3,600 deaths, specially during what is called 'The Troubles' in Northern Ireland between 1968 and the 1990s. In proportion to the population, if the Troubles had happened in the United Kingdom as a whole, then the number of deaths would have been over 137,000.

You can learn about this period in another textbook, *Troubled Images: The Northern Ireland Troubles and Peace Process 1968–2007*, by Gordon Gillespie, Colourpoint ISBN 978 1 904242 78 9.

Activity

1. Write out a list of all the counties in Ireland. For each one, find out one historical fact.

   It can be from any century, or even pre-history. For example:

   Co Cork — Michael Collins, leader of the IRA during the War of Independence, shot dead in 1922.

   Co Fermanagh — The mansion, Castle Coole, built between 1789 and 1798.

When you have done all you can, compare your list with others in the class.

How many different events have you found for each county?

You could make a display for your classroom wall, called "History in Irish counties".

Class Quiz!

Divide into two teams and decide on a prize for the winning team. If you get a question right, your team gets a point, BUT if you get a question wrong, you lose a point! So think carefully before you answer!

1. Who was the leader of the Easter Rising?

2. Who wrote, "Early this morning I signed my death warrant"?

3. In what year was the Anglo-Irish Treaty signed?

4. What were 'GI Brides'?

5. Name the nine counties of Ulster.

6. Name the three Treaty Ports.

7. After the Easter Rising, where were the rebels kept until they were executed?

8. Where were the headquarters of the rebels during the Easter Rising?

9. Complete this slogan: "England's difficulty is ...."

10. Why is the Irish flag sometimes called the Tricolour?

11. What is the full name of the parliament set up in Ireland in 1919?

12. What was the nickname for the reinforcements sent to help the police during the War of Independence?

13. What is the name and date of the Act which set up Northern Ireland as a six county state?

14. "Northern Ireland was never meant to be a permanent state." True or false?

15. Where was the first Parliament of Northern Ireland opened?

16. Who was the king at the time?

17. What happened to Parliament Buildings at Stormont during the Second World War and why?

18. Who was the first Prime Minister of Northern Ireland?

19. In what months and year was the Belfast Blitz?

20. Who was the British Prime Minister when the Anglo-Irish Treaty was signed?

Review this Unit

Look over this Unit again and make sure that you understand all that happened.

Discuss with your teacher any sections which you found difficult.

Has anything that you learned in this Unit come as a surprise to you?

Word Check

Check out these words to make sure you can spell them.

Pearse	Armagh	librarian
legacy	Fermanagh	Tyrone
partition	ambush	consequence
independence	Liffey	unification
Cobh	Dáil Eireann	controversial
Blitz	neutral	government
Monaghan	treaty	

If you're not sure if you can spell any of them, check them out a few more times.

BEFORE YOU START

How many methods of transport can you think of?

How many of these have you used?

Can you think of any ways of getting around which we don't use now? If you know a really old person, ask them what way they got to school when they were young. Ask them to tell you about their journey and how long it took. You might share this with the rest of the class.

People need to get around and they also need to transport the items they own or make. We'll look at the many ways to do this and we'll also see how many developments there were in transport during the twentieth century.

ON FOOT

The most basic form of transport is our own feet! At the beginning of the twentieth century, most ordinary people walked everywhere. Children walked to school even though it could be five miles or more away. Then they had to walk home again, no matter what the weather was like.
Poorer parents often couldn't buy shoes for their children and they went about barefoot. Sometimes children had shoes or boots but they were kept for special occasions so that they didn't wear out. In fact, you might be sent to school in bare feet but with your shoes hanging round your neck by the laces. When you were near the school, you stopped and put your shoes on for the day. You took them off again to walk home.

Activity

Look at this photograph. Make a list of differences between these children and how you dress for school.
What do you carry to school that these children do not have? Why might that be? What else do you notice in the photograph?

Parents who had a bit more money, or who were rich, were able to buy shoes and better clothes for their children. If your children went barefoot, it was a clear sign that you were working class.

There were children playing barefoot in some parts of Ireland right up to the 1950s.

Activity

Have you heard the saying "I'm going by shanks' mare"? (Some people might say "shanks' pony".) Do you know what this means?

If not, either

- look up this web site and find out:
  www.phrases.org.uk/meanings/shanks-mare.html
  or
- go to your library and find a big reference book called *Brewer's Dictionary of Phrase* and *Fable*. Look up the phrase in this book.

There is another phrase "The horse of ten toes". What do you think this refers to?

Activity

In groups, talk about walking everywhere and going without shoes. Remember that you have to do this at all times of the year, so you might have a different attitude depending on the season.

What could you do?

What could you not do?

What clothes would you need?

What would be good about it?

What would be bad about it?

What would you find most difficult about it?

Think about what it would mean for your daily life. For example, how long does it take you to get to school now? If you had to walk, how long would it take you? If you walk slowly, you will go at about two miles per hour. Walking fast is about four miles per hour.

Report back to the class.

Extended writing

Write a story about a girl or a boy (you choose!) who lives about 1910 and who walks to school in the nearest village every day. He or she has to cross a field and walk down country lanes. The family is poor but the child knows many of the people who live in the cottages along the way. Remember all the things you have read about walking in the early part of the twentieth century.

Plan your story:
Whose story will it be?
Give your character a name.
Plan how your character gets ready for school. What will he or she need to bring?
Will anyone else go with her?
What will happen along the way? This is the middle of your story and you can really use your imagination!
How will your story end?
Once you have your plan, write your story one stage at a time.

Perhaps the teacher will ask some of you to read out your stories, or perhaps they could be put up on the wall for everyone to read.

Review your work

Did you find this an easy exercise?
If you didn't, what did you find hard?
Do you feel you had enough information to write the story? If you feel you would have liked to know more, what information do you think would have made your story better?

BY THE WAY

Do you realise that there are people today who still have to walk many, many miles without shoes or sandals? Often they are carrying a child as well and maybe looking after another one too.
Where do you think this happens?
Why does it happen?

Here are pictures of something you still see on the doorstep of some bigger, older houses. It has something to do with walking. Can you guess what it is?
What does this tell you about the roads at the time?

Class discussion

Discuss whether we walk enough today.
How much walking do you do in a week?
Do you think you would be able to live without cars and buses and trains?

HORSE TRANSPORT

So people used their own feet to go places. But people could also use the feet on something else! At the beginning of the twentieth century, horses, ponies and donkeys were still an important part of everyday life for everybody.

BY THE WAY

Did you know that donkeys have a cross-shape of darker hair on their backs? You can clearly see it in these pictures.

Jesus rode into Jerusalem on a donkey and there is a legend that ever since that day all donkeys bear a cross on their backs.

Farmers used horses and donkeys for work round the farm. They pulled carts at harvest time to bring in the hay. Big cart horses were used to pull ploughs which turned over the soil so that the farmer could sow his crops.

Research

There are some people who want to keep things from the past and continue the way life was many years ago. Here is a photograph (right), of an Amish farmer who still uses horses to pull machinery in his fields. This picture could have been taken a hundred years ago but in fact it was taken in Ohio in 2008.

Find out more about the Amish people, such as where they live and what they believe.

Present your findings as a bullet-pointed list.

At the end, write a paragraph explaining what you think of the Amish way of life and whether you think they should accept a more modern lifestyle.

What might they gain if they adopted modern ways?

What might they lose?

Families would also use horse drawn vehicles to go to town, visit each other or go to church. In some country churches there were stables where the horses were kept while the service was taking place. Sometimes the horses might have been put out into a field beside the church to graze until it was time to go home.

In some terraces today you will see arched entrances like the one below. This was to let horse drawn vehicles into a courtyard at the back of the house.

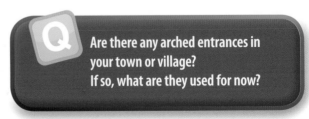

Q Are there any arched entrances in your town or village?
If so, what are they used for now?

This archway is in the main street of Newtownards, Co Down.

Activity

Unlike a car or a lorry, a horse is a living creature. When many horses were used every day there were occupations associated with looking after them and the carriages, wagons and carts that they pulled. Looking after horses provided a lot of employment.

Write out each of these occupations and pick the correct meaning from the list on the right.

Blacksmith   … made saddles and harnesses for horses

Stabler   … looked after a family's carriage and often drove it

Saddler   … took care of the horses' stables, cleaned them, fed the horses etc.

Wheelwright   … kept stables where people could pay to have their horses looked after

Coachman   … made wheels for carts

Groom   … worked in a forge and made horseshoes and other iron items

A cartwheel.

The rim of the wheel is covered by an iron hoop. What problems might a blacksmith face when making a hoop like this?

Activity

Here is a picture of a blacksmith working in his forge.

On your own, write a description of this forge. Comment on as many things as you can. What tools can you identify? Include details of what it would be like to work here every day. Write *at least 100* words.

Now compare your description with that of a partner. Has your partner noticed things that you didn't notice? Did you comment on things that your partner didn't? Why do you think that was?

Horses and War

Horses have been used on the battlefield in wartime. Armies had cavalry units that took part in charges against the enemy. Horses were also used to pull artillery. In the First World War, over 8 million horses were killed and two and a half million were injured.

Here is a picture of horses pulling artillery in the First World War.

LINK TO FIRST WORLD WAR UNIT

William Butler Yeats, the famous Irish poet, died in 1939. He wrote an inscription to be put on his gravestone. Here is a picture of his gravestone, in Drumcliff Churchyard, Co Sligo.

MA

TPD

BC

INSCRIPTION: a short special message, often cut into a hard surface like stone, metal or wood.

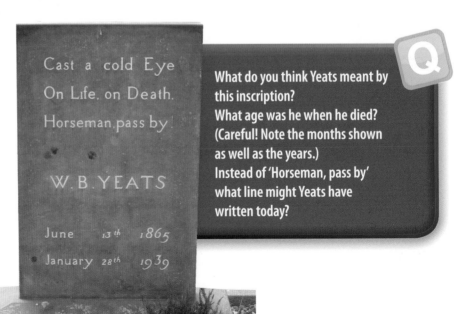

Cast a cold Eye
On Life, on Death.
Horseman, pass by!

W.B. YEATS

June 13th 1865
January 28th 1939

Q

What do you think Yeats meant by this inscription?
What age was he when he died? (Careful! Note the months shown as well as the years.)
Instead of 'Horseman, pass by' what line might Yeats have written today?

Thinking about change

The Fintona Horse Tram

Fintona in Co Tyrone was home to a very famous tram which was pulled by a horse.

The Fintona Horse Tram was the last horse tram in the British Isles to operate an all-year-round service. It was also the longest serving horse tramway in the world.

Fintona railway station was about 1100 metres outside the town and a short branch line was built to carry passengers to and from the station.

There was an earlier tram, but the tram in the photograph below came into service in 1883 and was still running when the line finally closed on 30 September 1957.

Photographers came from all over the world to take pictures of it. Here is a photograph taken about 1914.

What do you think of this picture?

Describe what you see.

Is there anything more you would like to know? If you could talk to one of the station staff in this picture, what would you ask them?

What jobs might these men do? For example one of them is probably the tram driver.

A large cart horse was needed to pull the tram and over the years there were many horses used. Each horse pulled the tram every day for about 10 or 12 years. No matter whether the horse was male or female, it was always called 'Dick'!

In the 1950s many of the railways in Ulster were closed, including the one that served Fintona. The government realised that the railway network needed to be modernised, but this would be very expensive, specially in rural areas. So they decided to use only buses for public transport in most areas of Northern Ireland.
With no railway, there was no more need for the horse tram.

RURAL: to do with the countryside

121

Read the following extract carefully. It is from a book called *The Fintona Horse Tram*, by Norman Johnston. Answer the questions that follow.

"The fate of the horse became a big issue in the town when the closure of the line was confirmed. Dick was virtually a mascot to Fintona, and many people wanted him to stay in the town… In the last week Tom Bradley [the Station Master] had about a hundred phone calls from England asking, "What is going to happen to Dick?" Tom replied, "To Dick? What's going to happen to Tom?" Nobody thought of what would happen to the station staff!

The big fear was that the horse might be put down because in the 1950s there was no market for redundant, 15 year old cart horses. All over the British Isles horse drawn carts and delivery vehicles were giving way to lorries and vans. On the farm it was just the same. The tractor was ousting the horse.

Most redundant horses ended up at the knacker's yard. Worse still, French buyers were coming to the horse fairs and markets and buying up large numbers of horses cheaply… The poor horses ended up as dog meat.

In the last week of September 1957, the *Ulster Herald* carried the following advertisement:

The Great Northern Railway Board has for sale one black horse, age approximately 15 years, which may be inspected at Fintona Station.

… Unexpectedly it was announced that the Ulster Society for the Prevention of Cruelty to Animals (USPCA) had purchased Dick for £45. This was part of a wider policy by the USPCA at this time, of buying up horses, ponies and donkeys which were destined for the slaughter house."

Dick retired to a farm in Seskinore, near Fintona.

1. Why do you think people were more worried about the horse that about the station staff?

2. Do you think the writer is sympathetic to the horse? Quote from the passage to support your opinion.

3. Write out a list of people or things affected by the closure of the railway and horse tram. Beside each one, say how they were

affected. For example, "School children: they couldn't go to school by train any more." Then say what else could be done instead, for example, "School children could go to school by bus."

4. When there is change, often people lose their jobs. Should all the railway staff at Fintona have lost their jobs in 1957? Examine alternatives to this course of action and look at the financial implications of anything you suggest.

Activity

This a memory from a woman who lived in Fintona when she was a child. (The 'junction' she refers to is the railway station. It was called Fintona Junction.)

"My mum, brother and sisters remember playing on the platforms on the junction itself. Still to this day when I go up to visit my granda we can walk the railway line. I never honestly knew myself that it was such a big part of history."

This woman had no idea that she was seeing a part of history. Is there anything that you have lived through that you think people will be learning about in history lessons in the future? If so, explain what it is and why you think people will remember it.

Activity

Colour in a picture of the Fintona Horse Tram. You could put your pictures up on the wall of your classroom.

Activity

Find out more about the Fintona Horse Tram.
Either
Make a wall display for your classroom. Include pictures and word processed captions and short articles.
Or
In groups, put together a presentation on the Fintona Horse Tram. Decide who will research each aspect of your study. Finish with a study of the changes that affected the town of Fintona. Use a software program to illustrate your presentation. Each person in the group should contribute.

Sources:

Books — *The Fintona Horse Tram* by Norman Johnston, West Tyrone Historical Society, 1992, ISBN 0 9517175 1 0
Irish Trams by Jim Kilroy, Colourpoint Books, 1996
ISBN 1 898392 02 1
Both these books are now out of print, but you may be able to find copies in your library.
Use a search engine. This will bring up many links.

Go to see the tram! Dick retired to a farm but the tram itself can still be seen because it is preserved in the Ulster Folk and Transport Museum at Cultra, outside Belfast. If you are close enough, you could take a trip to the Transport Galleries in the Museum and, as well as the Fintona Horse Tram, you will see many real examples of early transport of all types. The museum web site is www.uftm.org.uk/

Review your work

Were you happy with the presentation your group gave?

What comments did others in the class make about your presentation?

Do you agree with their comments? Why or why not?

If you were doing it again, what would you do differently?

BY THE WAY

'ISBN' stands for 'International Standard Book Number'. It is a unique number given to every edition of a book. It is used for all sorts of records to do with the book. For example, books are listed by ISBN in a bookshop and the barcode representing the ISBN is scanned at the till when you buy a book. What is the ISBN of this book?

UNIQUE: the only one of its kind.

TIP
 PROJECT
 BEFORE YOU START
 ACTIVITY
 BY THE WAY
 SOURCES
WORD BOX
LINK
 RESEARCH

BICYCLES

Imagine if you have always had to walk everywhere or use horse transport. Then someone invents a mode of transport that doesn't need to be fed or stabled or groomed every day. The invention of the bicycle meant great freedom to travel short distances. The bicycle was around in the nineteenth century but the shape of bicycle that we know today developed just before 1900.

This is a bicycle from the late nineteenth century. It is called a '**penny-farthing**'. Why do you think it is called this?

Look at this bicycle carefully. Where is the saddle? Where are the pedals? The rubber tyres were solid, not like the tyres today, which are filled with air. There are straight handlebars but you can't see them very well in this photograph.

Can you work out how you would mount this bicycle? The saddle was about 1.5 meters off the ground. It wasn't easy – and it was just as hard to dismount! Men found it easier to ride because they wore trousers and could be more energetic in public than women could! What do you think it would be like to ride it?

 Q

 LINK TO MONEY UNIT

By 1900, the bicycle looked much like it does today. Because it was safer to ride, these early bikes were called 'safety bicycles'.

This is a bicycle made about 1900. What do you think of it?

What do you notice about the way the man is dressed?

Do you think it would be easy for a woman in long skirts to ride this bicycle? Why or why not?

Q

At first bicycles were quite expensive and cycling was an activity only for those who could afford it. By the 1930s, bicycles were cheaper and more people were able to afford them. For the first time, ordinary working class people were able to travel farther.

Class discussion

Here is what one old woman remembered about living on a farm in Fermanagh in the 1930s. She had got a job and was able to afford a bicycle. A 'trap' was a light wooden horse-drawn vehicle.

"My mother wasn't able to go anywhere off the farm very easily. If she wanted to go into Lisnaskea to do some messages she had to get out the trap and get the pony hitched up and that could take a while. Once I got my bicycle, I could just hop on it and get the messages in half the time."

Talk about the difference it made to a farming family in a rural area like Fermanagh once the bicycle made transport cheaper and easier.

Q What were the advantages of using a pony and trap?
What were the disadvantages of using a bicycle?

BY THE WAY

Bloomers were named after an American suffragette, Amelia Bloomer (1818–1894).She had seen the 'trousers' worn by fashionable Turkish ladies in Istanbul and thought they were a great idea.

Women and bicycles

The invention of the safety bicycle had a great effect on the lives of women. There were several reasons for this.

For the first time, women were able to get about on their own without needing men to look after horses and stables and coaches and wagons and so on. It was possible to walk out the door, get on a bicycle and go into town or visit a neighbour without needing to tell anyone else.

This had a great impact on the suffragette movement of the late nineteenth and early twentieth century. Women felt a much greater sense of independence and personal freedom and were able to attend meetings and demonstrations whenever they wanted. One woman called the bicycle 'the freedom machine'.

Cycling also caused a change in the way women dressed. Wearing tight corsets didn't help with freedom of movement and long skirts got tangled in the wheels and pedals. So divided skirts and 'bloomers' were invented.

Activity

Look at these two comments.

"Have you ever seen anything more off-putting, uglier, meaner than a wench on a bike, wheezing, her face red like a turkey, her eyes reddened by the dust? I haven't… What a horror! Is there any element of beauty to such a furious dame on wheels? Cycling makes our women haggard and angular, unwomanly from the out and the inside. Off your bikes, female sex! Or you will no longer enjoy the right to call your sex the fair one!"

A journalist writing in a magazine in 1897

EMANCIPATE: make free

UNTRAMMELLED: not bound by anything

1. Look at Source a. Select adjectives in the source that highlight the negative side of cycling.

2. Do you think the journalist is male or female? Give reasons for your answer.

3. What do you think may influence the opinions of the journalist?

b "Let me tell you what I think of bicycling. I think it has done more to emancipate women than anything else in the world. It gives women a feeling of freedom and self-reliance. I stand and rejoice every time I see a woman ride by on a wheel… the picture of free, untrammelled womanhood."

Susan B Anthony, an American suffragette

1 Pick out three benefits for women described by this writer.

2. Give reasons why a suffragette would support an independent means of travel.

Activity

Write a letter to the magazine (Source a) explaining why you agree or disagree with the journalist's opinion.

CAPTION COMPETITION!

One of the two women in this cartoon is a cyclist. Can you tell which one? How can you tell?

Think up a caption. Write down all the suggestions from your class. Then have a vote for the best one. Maybe you could have a prize!

On a computer, make a poster of the cartoon and put the winning caption on it. Display this in your classroom.

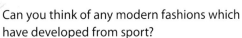

Can you think of any modern fashions which have developed from sport?

Look at this cartoon. It was published in a US magazine called *Puck*, in 1897.

What do you think the cartoonist is trying to say?

Justify your conclusions by referring to the cartoon and linking it to what you have learnt.

Do you think cartoons are useful as a way of making a point?

Class Quiz!

Divide into two teams and decide on a prize for the winning team. If you get a question right, your team gets a point, BUT if you get a question wrong, you lose a point!

1. What form of transport doesn't have any wheels?
2. What is an ISBN?
3. What is the legend about the cross-shape on a donkey's back?
4. Who was Amelia Bloomer?
5. How did a penny-farthing get its name?
6. What was called a 'freedom machine?
7. There were no bicycles before 1900. True or false?
8. Which is the odd one out and why — horse tram, bicycle, foot, pony and trap?
9. Name a reference book where you can look up the origins of sayings.
10. Who was WB Yeats?
11. What does 'I'm going by Shanks' mare' mean?
12. What sort of horse was used to pull a plough?
13. What does a saddler do?
14. In which county is Fintona?
15. What was the name of the horse that pulled the Fintona tram?
16. Who makes horseshoes?

Word Check

Check out these words to make sure you can spell them.

wheelwright	**character**	**artillery**
carriage	**stories**	**Yeats**
clothes	**terrace**	**vehicle**
ordinary	**forge**	**slaughter**
dictionary	**description**	**junction**
attitude	**residential**	**museum**
either	**surrounding**	

If you're not sure if you can spell any of them, check them out a few more times.

This is a photograph of Royal Avenue in Belfast, taken about 1900.
What do you see in this picture?
How many forms of transport can you see?
What forms of transport do you not see?
What do you think the parallel lines on the road are?

BEFORE YOU START

Up until the nineteenth century (1800s) people moved around either on foot or by using private transport. By the middle of the 1800s *public* transport began to develop. If you walked down a street in a city in Ireland or Britain in 1900, you would still have seen plenty of people walking and there would be horse-drawn carts and coaches, but there would also be bicycles, trams and perhaps a railway station where you could catch a train.

The Railways

The nineteenth century had seen the invention and development of travel using steam locomotives on railway lines. By 1900 there was a large network of railways in Britain and Ireland.

Activity

Study these two maps and then answer the questions that follow.

The railway network in Ulster in 1906.

The railway network today.

1. In 1906, was it possible to go from Belfast to Strabane by train?

2. "I live in Enniskillen today. I can go to see my grandparents in Portadown by train." True or false?

3. Are there any railways in County Tyrone today?

4. What is the name of the small island off the north coast?

5. Were there ever any railways on the Ards Peninsula in the twentieth century?

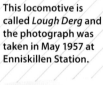

This locomotive is called *Lough Derg* and the photograph was taken in May 1957 at Enniskillen Station.

6. Why do you think the railways in the east of Ulster are still there?

At the beginning of the twentieth century, all trains were pulled by steam locomotives. Steam locomotives are powered by coal, which heats water to make steam. Here is a picture of a steam locomotive that first ran in Ireland in 1915.

For how many years had it been running when the picture was taken?

Steam power gave way to diesel in the 1950s. Here is a picture of a diesel train.

This diesel train is photographed at Clones in Co Cavan in April 1956.

Questions

Look at the pictures of the two trains.

- What similarities do they have?

- How are they different?

- Which do you thinks looks best?

- Do you think they sound different as they move?

- Which looks the cleanest?

- What do you notice about the dates of the two photographs? What can you conclude from this?

- Could pictures of trains be taken in these towns now?

CONCLUDE: come to a decision based on evidence

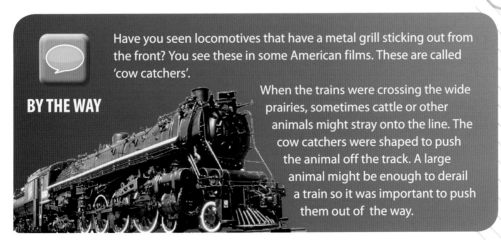

BY THE WAY

Have you seen locomotives that have a metal grill sticking out from the front? You see these in some American films. These are called 'cow catchers'.

When the trains were crossing the wide prairies, sometimes cattle or other animals might stray onto the line. The cow catchers were shaped to push the animal off the track. A large animal might be enough to derail a train so it was important to push them out of the way.

Railways and the local community

Railways were a very important method of transport up until the 1920s. There weren't many cars around before then because they were still being developed and were very expensive. Bicycles were fine for going short distances but you couldn't go from Belfast to Dublin on one very quickly!

Do you know what a 'commuter' is? If not, look it up and write out what it means in your own words.

Railways brought significant changes to society. These changes affected both the towns and the countryside.

For the first time, it meant that ordinary people could live farther away from their place of work. If they were near a railway, they could just get a train to work. This meant that more houses could be built further out of the towns, and even in nearby towns. For example, once there was a railway from Belfast to Bangor in County Down, people who worked in Belfast could live in Bangor. These people were **commuters**.

FREIGHT: goods being transported

Activity

Draw a spider diagram about the effect of railways on the population.

You could start like this:

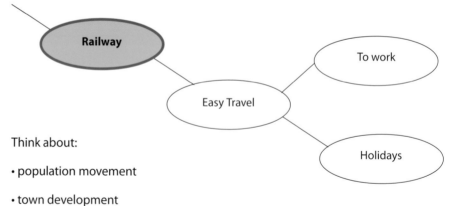

Think about:

• population movement

• town development

• housing

• holidays

• the movement of freight

The railways gave house builders an idea. To encourage families to buy a house in a town like Bangor or Whitehead, they would offer a free 'Villa Ticket' to the buyer. This was a season ticket for the train into Belfast, valid for possibly a number of years. So if you bought a house in Bangor, you would have free travel to work every day.

TIP

PROJECT

BEFORE YOU START

ACTIVITY

BY THE WAY

SOURCES

WORD BOX

LINK

RESEARCH

Activity

There were three different people involved in the Villa Ticket system:

• the house builder

• the railway

• the house buyer

Write two sentences on each one, saying how they each benefited from the Villa Ticket system.

The railway station was an important focal point in a country community.

Remember that in the first decades of the twentieth century there were very few cars around.

The railway station in a village gave employment to quite a few people.

If you wanted to send a parcel, you could take it to the railway station and send it by train. You might go to the station to collect a parcel that was being sent to you.

If someone was coming to see you, you might go to the station to collect them from the train.

If you were travelling somewhere yourself, you would probably catch a train.

Activity

Look at this picture.

This train is stopped near Kiltubrid on the Cavan and Leitrim Railway. It is March 1959.

What do you think is happening?

The guard is leaning out of a carriage window talking to another man. What do you think they are looking at?

There are three forms of transport in this scene. Can you spot them all?

Use your imagination to write two or three paragraphs based on this picture. Imagine who the people on the road are and why they have come to meet the train.

With the coming of the railways, ordinary people were able to go away for a day out. This was not possible before. Whole families could take a day at the seaside.

Can you imagine what it must have been like to be able to see the sea for the very first time? Not only that, but you could actually bathe in the sea for the first time!

It might seem hard to imagine, but railways were the main reason that ordinary working people were able to take a proper holiday for the first time.

 What effect do you think this had on seaside towns?

Activity

Design a railway poster encouraging people to go on holiday to Portrush.

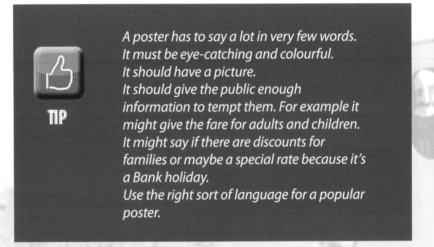

TIP

A poster has to say a lot in very few words. It must be eye-catching and colourful. It should have a picture. It should give the public enough information to tempt them. For example it might give the fare for adults and children. It might say if there are discounts for families or maybe a special rate because it's a Bank holiday. Use the right sort of language for a popular poster.

Research

COM
ICT
MI
TPD
BC
WO

The *Flying Scotsman* is one of the most famous steam locomotives in the British Isles. It was named after the long-distance, non-stop, passenger train which it hauled. See how much you can find out about this locomotive (not the train service).

For example:

- What cities did it travel between?
- When was it built?
- How much did it cost to make?
- It was designed by a famous locomotive engineer. Who was he?
- Where is it now?
- Can you find a picture of it?

Work on your own, in pairs or as a group.

TIP

PROJECT

BEFORE YOU START

ACTIVITY

BY THE WAY

SOURCES

WORD BOX

LINK

RESEARCH

You could present your findings as a word processed report;
or
You could put together an audio visual presentation;
or
You could make a display for your classroom.
Whichever option you choose, you must word-process an account of how you went about your research. What did you do first?
You must note down where you got each piece of your information. These are your sources.

After the 1920s, the railways began to decline. There were several reasons for this.

1. During the First World War employers found it harder to find people to work for them because so many men were away fighting. Also many were killed and would never return home. When labour is scarce, wages have to go up in order to attract workers. When the war was over, it was impossible to bring wages down again because people had got used to them. In fact, wages trebled after the war. The higher wage became the rate for the job.

2. In 1920, the government introduced the eight hour working day. If an employer wanted a worker to work longer than that, he had to pay overtime. Before this, a signalman might have been employed for 13 hours at a basic rate of pay. Now the railway had to pay him 5 hours overtime or else employ a second signalman.

3. Buses and lorries were now on the roads, taking more and more passengers and freight off the railways. The roads were strong competition for the railways.

4. When Ireland was divided when the border was set up in 1921, many of the railways were split between the two states. This became very difficult to maintain and some railways were closed.

LINK TO FIRST WORLD WAR UNIT

LINK TO SECOND IRELAND UNIT

Activity

Role-play a discussion between two railway managers in 1929. They are examining the difficulties the railway faces and looking at the implications. Can they come up with alternatives to combat the adverse conditions?

ADVERSE: unfavourable

Research

In developing countries, or in areas of the world where people are very poor, public transport is very important.

Investigate public transport in one of the following places:

India
China
Kenya
New York

Is it very different to what you are used to here?

How and why is it different?

> **OPINION TIME!**
>
> "Give us back our lost railways!" Discuss this in class. Should closed railways in Ulster be re-opened?
>
> Are they better than cars and lorries for passenger and freight transport?

Try this!

> Percy French (1854–1920) was a famous Irish songwriter. He was born in Co Roscommon and went to Foyle College in Derry. One of his most famous songs is "Are Ye Right there, Michael?" This was a humorous song about the West Clare Railway.
>
> Find the words of this song and sing it in class.

Trams and Buses

In the picture at the beginning of this Unit on page 129, the vehicle in the right foreground is a horse tram. Trams are vehicles that run on rails, a bit like trains, but tram rails are set into the road and trams share the road with everyone else. Did you guess correctly what the lines on the road were?

Belfast, Derry, Dublin and Cork had horse trams.

Electricity

When electricity began to be used widely, many things about everyday life changed. Today we take electricity so much for granted that it is hard for us to imagine life without it.

Activity

Go on an imaginary walk round your house. In each room, note down everything that uses electricity. Remember that things that use batteries are using the electricity stored in those batteries.

Think about what life would be like without all these items. What could you do instead? For example, if there were no vacuum cleaners, you would have to brush and sweep much more and maybe get down on your hands and knees to clean the floors by hand.

What about your mobile phone? Do you have an MP3 player? Would you miss these items if, suddenly, there was no electricity any more?

Of all the electrical items you have thought of, which would you miss most? Why?

Think of the others in your family. Which item do you think each of them would miss most?

The use of electricity as a source of power developed quite slowly at first during the nineteenth century, but by the beginning of the twentieth century some industries had installed electric generators in their factories to power their machines and to provide lighting.

Once there was electric lighting, you could see very well even after the sun had set. Gas lamps were useful for small areas, but needed to be lit and maintained. You couldn't have a very good gaelic or rugby match in the evening if it was lit only by gas lamps round the pitch!

As well as industry, owners of large houses and stately homes installed electric generators, mainly to provide lighting. It was an exciting development and families were very proud to be able to boast that they had electric light!

In the 1950s, some hotels made a point of advertising that they had 'running water and electric light'.

Electricity was much slower reaching rural areas. There were parts of Northern Ireland where houses in the country still had no electricity in the 1960s.

Questions

Private generators are still used in some places today, specially where a back-up electricity supply is needed in case the main power supply is cut.

Can you think of places that may have back-up generators? Why do they need them?

What did these places do before they had an electricity supply?

In the 1890s, electricity began to be generated on a commercial level in Northern Ireland, although on a very small scale. At first it was used mainly for street lighting.

Then more uses for it began to be found and in 1905, Belfast went over to electric trams.

Questions

Why do you think the horse trams were replaced by electric trams?

How did this affect (i) the horses (ii) the drivers of the horse trams (iii) the streets?

Derry kept the horse trams until 1919 and then went over to diesel buses a bit like we have today.

BY THE WAY Buses in Londonderry have to have particularly strong engines because there are so many steep hills in the city.
There can be no double-deckers on Derry City bus routes either. Can you think why?

Electric wires were hung over the streets on the tram routes and a pole from the roof of the tram took electricity from these wires. You can see this in the picture on page 140.

As the century went on, more and more cars were appearing on the roads. This meant that trams and cars got in each other's way sometimes.

TIP

PROJECT

BEFORE YOU START

ACTIVITY

BY THE WAY

SOURCES

WORD BOX

LINK

RESEARCH

Activity

Penny debate

It is 1908. Read these facts:

- Trams had to travel on rails. If a new route was planned, the road had to be dug up to lay the tram rails. Poles had to be erected to carry the electricity.

- Electric trams could not pull into the pavement, out of the way of the other traffic, to pick up passengers. Passengers had to walk out into the road to get onto the tram.

- In the earlier days of trams there weren't many cars on the roads.

- Trams could carry a lot of people at one time.

- Cars and bicycles could get caught in the tram rails. One man recalled: "I turned out onto the Lisburn road and my car wheels slotted into the electric tram rails. They were an exact fit! There was a tram coming straight for me. I really had to struggle to get the wheels turned to jump out of the rails before the tram reached me. It was a scary moment!"

Divide the class into three groups.

One group is in favour of travel by tram.

The second group is in favour of travel by the new invention, the motor car.

The third group must listen carefully to the debate but not join in.

Give each person in the first two groups three pennies each.

Using all the information they have read as well as their own ideas, the first two groups should have a discussion. Each group is trying to persuade the other that their method of transport is better.

Rules: Only one person can speak at one time.

No-one should speak for more than one minute at a time.

As soon as you have spoken, you must give up one of your pennies. When you have no pennies left, you can't say any more, no matter how much you would like to!

So you must think carefully about what you say and how you say it.

At the end of the debate, the third group should vote on who they think won the argument. Each person in the third group should give their reasons for the way they voted.

Before you finish up, talk about the debate. Did anyone feel that they didn't express themselves well?

Did anyone have more to say even after he or she had no pennies left?

Did you find it hard to stay silent when someone was saying something you didn't agree with?

Trolley buses were introduced in Belfast in 1938. Trolley buses were a bit like trams except that they didn't run on rails. They had rubber tyres and could be driven anywhere without needing rails to be laid in the road.

Belfast had the largest trolley bus system in the UK, apart from London. The streets were criss-crossed with overhead electric power lines and two poles from the roof of the trolley bus were attached to these power lines

This photograph was taken at a gate into Parliament Buildings at Stormont. You can see all the trolley bus overhead wires.

When an historian is trying to date a photograph, sometimes he can conclude only that it must have been taken between two dates. Think of two things that might help an historian to date this photograph.

This trolley bus was photographed on the Falls Road route about the middle of the 1960s. Can you see the poles going up to the wires from the roof of the bus?

The last trolley buses were withdrawn from service by 1968 as the bus service gradually changed over to diesel vehicles.

CHANGE THROUGH TIME

Cars

At the beginning of the twentieth century, cars were just being developed. There had been many attempts to make vehicles that were self-propelled. Some of these were huge steam machines that could go at only two miles per hour! The first people to experiment successfully with petrol engine vehicles were Gottlieb Daimler and Karl Benz in Germany in the 1880s.

At first the speed limit was twelve miles per hour, although this was raised to 20 miles per hour in 1903. This was much too slow for King Edward VII who, in 1906, was driven by his chauffeur along the London to Brighton road at 60 miles per hour!

Look at the photographs of cars on this and the following pages.

> **SELF-PROPELLED:** able to move without being pulled or pushed by something else

This car was made about 1904

A 6hp single cylinder Mobile two seater.

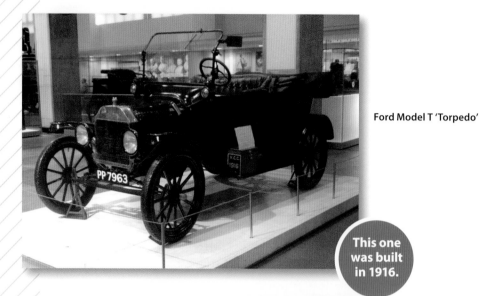

Ford Model T 'Torpedo'

This one was built in 1916.

Austin 12 'Windsor'

This one was built in 1927.

Rover 16

This one was built about 1937.

This one was built about 1950

Wolseley 6/80

This one was built about 1966

Triumph 2000

Ford Escort Popular Plus

This one was built in 1975.

Activity

Study each of the car pictures, one at a time.

Write about 60 words on each one. What do you notice about each model? For example, the car built around 1950 has a split windscreen. What reason could there be for this?

Now look at the development of the car. What has changed as you go from picture to picture through the century? Has anything remained the same?

Between which two models do you think there was the biggest change?

Early cars had solid rubber tyres but later on, pneumatic tyres were used. This change was necessary mainly because of the rise in the speed limit. Solid tyres are all right for slow speeds but passengers were rattled to bits at higher speeds! This was specially true because the roads weren't as smooth as they are now and many town and city streets were still cobbled. Pneumatic tyres absorb more of the bumps.

BY THE WAY

The pneumatic tyre was invented by John Boyd Dunlop (1840–1921). He was Scottish and trained as a veterinary surgeon. In 1867 he moved to Belfast.
His son was finding it very uncomfortable riding his solid-wheeled tricycle on the cobblestones and this made Dunlop look for an alternative. Today Dunlop Tyres is still a major company.
A portrait of John Dunlop appears on Northern Bank £10 notes.

Q What age was Dunlop when he moved to Belfast?

Q Think of two reasons why he might have moved there.

Activity

In pairs, imagine that it is 1906 and one of you has just come back from town. You have just seen a motor car for the very first time. Describe what you have seen to your partner. What are your feelings at seeing this vehicle? Remember that you have never before seen any vehicle move without being pulled or pushed by an animal or a person. You have to try to get your partner to imagine what it was like. Your partner must try to draw what you are describing.

Underneath the picture, write down the main impressions you have of this new vehicle. What did it sound like? Were there any smells coming from it? How was the driver dressed?

What difference will this new mode of transport make to the roads around you? Will anything change? Will anything *have* to change?

TIP

PROJECT

BEFORE YOU START

ACTIVITY

BY THE WAY

SOURCES

WORD BOX

LINK

RESEARCH

Chambers Cars

For more than twenty years in the early days of motoring, Belfast had its own car manufacturing company. Chambers Motors Ltd of Belfast was set up in 1904. It was founded by three brothers and made high quality cars. In all, the company made about 2000 vehicles. During the First World War, Chambers made ambulances for the Ulster Division of the army.

The company was unable to survive the competition from other car makers who used mass production methods to make cars much more quickly and more cheaply. Chambers Cars had to close in 1927.

Here is a photograph of a Chambers car which you can see in the Ulster Museum in Belfast.

A 10 hp Chambers Open Tourer, believed to have been made in 1906.

There are only four preserved Chambers cars left in the world.

LINK TO MONEY UNIT

Research
DeLorean Motor Company

Northern Ireland had another motor car manufacturer, the DeLorean Motor Company.

It was set up in 1975.

Your task is to find information on this company and the car that it manufactured.

Find out:

• who set it up
• where it was located
• what events were taking place in Northern Ireland at this time
• why the factory was built in Northern Ireland
• what sort of car DeLorean built and what it looked like
• what was different about its doors
• when the company closed and why
• in what films a DeLorean car features

Remember to keep a note of your sources!

When you have found all your information, write an outline for a feature for your local newspaper on the history of the DeLorean Motor Company.

Under your outline headings, make notes on what detail you will include in each paragraph.

Once you are happy with your outline, write and illustrate your article.

COM
ICT
MI
TPD
BC

A line-up of new DeLorean cars.

Activity

Draw a picture of a DeLorean car. Try drawing it with its doors open!

....

Look at the picture of a Belfast street on page 41. You can see how empty it is of cars. Cars were only for better off people right up until the 1930s and even then not all middle class people could afford them. There was a good market for second-hand cars. It wasn't until the late 1950s that cars became more affordable for ordinary working people.

Activity

As cars began to be more easily purchased by ordinary people, this new form of private transport changed many things in every day life. Draw a mind map of the effect of cars on the countryside, towns and cities, places that were not used to them.

Start like this:

Remember that some things can be both advantages *and* disadvantages. For example, although the need to surface roads gave employment, it also used up space in the countryside and farmers lost good agricultural land.

....

Air travel

The year 1900 is generally regarded as the beginning of the pioneering era in successful air flight. There had been many attempts before this, such as hot-air balloons, but none were really sustainable as controlled ways of travel.

One of the first machines to be tried successfully was the airship. These were called **Zeppelins** after the person who developed them, Ferdinand von Zeppelin, who was German. Airships were lighter-than-air aircraft because they were filled with a gas, such as hydrogen, which enabled them to fly. They could also be propelled and steered.

Airships could be huge. The small section with windows on the underside of this airship is the passenger compartment.

They were extremely smooth in flight and sometimes passengers went to sleep and didn't realise they had taken off.

Passengers could walk around, have a meal, listen to live music and gaze out the windows.

One of the most famous air accidents of the twentieth century involved an airship called the **Hindenburg**.

This picture shows how spacious the cabin of the *Hindenburg* was.

The *Hindenburg* had flown across the Atlantic and was landing in New Jersey in the United States on Thursday 6 May, 1937. Airships 'docked' at a mooring mast by dropping ropes and being tethered.

When the *Hindenburg* was still about 300 feet up, a burst of flame was seen near the rear of the ship. Because the airship was made of very light material and filled with gas, the fire engulfed the entire ship rapidly. It took only 34 seconds for the whole airship to burn completely and crash to the ground in a ball of fire.

ENGULF: completely overwhelm.

This picture shows the moments after the fire started.

Thirty-six people died, which was remarkably few, considering the scale of the fire.

A radio journalist, Herbert Morrison, was giving a live commentary of the *Hindenburg* landing. This is what he said:

" *It's practically standing still now. They've dropped ropes out of the nose of the ship; and (uh) they've been taken hold of down on the field by a number of men. It's starting to rain again; it's—the rain had (uh) slacked up a little bit. The back motors of the ship are just holding it (uh) just enough to keep it from— It's burst into flames! It burst into flames, and it's falling, it's crashing! Watch it! Watch it! Get out of the way! Get out of the way! Get this, Charlie; get this, Charlie! It's fire—and it's crashing! It's crashing terrible! Oh, my! Get out of the way, please! It's burning and bursting into flames; and the—and it's falling on the mooring-mast. And all the folks agree that this is terrible; this is the one of the worst catastrophes in the world. [indecipherable] its flames... Crashing, oh! Four- or five-hundred feet into the sky and it—it's a terrific crash, ladies and gentlemen. It's smoke, and it's in flames now; and the frame is crashing to the ground, not quite to the mooring-mast. Oh, the humanity! and all the passengers screaming around here. I told you; it—I can't even talk to people Their friends are out there! Ah! It's—it—it's a— ah! I—I can't talk, ladies and gentlemen. Honest: it's just laying there, mass of smoking wreckage. Ah! And everybody can hardly breathe and talk and the screaming. Lady, I—I—I'm sorry. Honest: I—I can hardly breathe. I—I'm going to step inside, where I cannot see it. Charlie, that's terrible. Ah, ah;—I can't. Listen, folks; I—I'm gonna have to stop for a minute because [indecipherable] I've lost my voice. This is the worst thing I've ever witnessed.*"

Herbert Morrison, describing the events, as broadcasted to WLS radio.

This description of the disaster as it happened is an important record. You can hear the actual recording on this web site:

history1900s.about.com/gi/o.htm?zi=1/XJ&zu=http%3A//www.eyewitnesstohistory.com/vohind.htm

Q

1. At what point in Herbert Morrison's commentary does his tone change?

2. What would you say his mood was before the *Hindenburg* caught fire? How can you tell?

3. What do you think Morrison means by "Get this, Charlie; get this, Charlie!"? He mentions Charlie again later. Who might Charlie be?

4. Is this commentary a primary or a secondary source? Explain your answer.

AVIATOR: pilot of an aircraft.

The *Daily Mail* newspaper was responsible for some developments in early man-powered flight. Between 1907 and 1930, the paper offered prizes for various achievements. In 1908, it offered a prize of £1000 for the first flight across the English Channel. Louis Blériot (a French engineer and aviator) succeeded in June 1909 in a flight from near Calais in France to Dover in England. This prize money would be worth about £55,000 today.

In 1918, the *Daily Mail* newspaper offered a prize of £10,000 to "the aviator who shall first cross the Atlantic in an aeroplane in flight from any point in the United States of America, Canada or Newfoundland to any point in Great Britain or Ireland in 72 consecutive hours".

Here is a notice about the prize in a newsletter of the Royal Aero Club of the United Kingdom, 21 November 1918.

THE *DAILY MAIL* ATLANTIC PRIZE.

Now that the Royal Aero Club, with the advent of the Armistice, has officially notified all those whom it may concern that the *Daily Mail* Prize for an Atlantic crossing, *via* the air, is now again open for competition, we re-print the rules governing this prize, as no doubt there are many who may not have in mind all the clauses and their bearing.

The Proprietors of the *Daily Mail* have offered the sum of £10,000 to be awarded to the aviator who shall first cross the Atlantic in an aeroplane in flight from any point in the United States, Canada, or Newfoundland to any point in Great Britain or Ireland, in 72 consecutive hours. The flight may be made either way across the Atlantic

General

1. A competitor, by entering, thereby agrees that he is bound by the regulations herein contained or to be hereafter issued in connection with this competition.

2. The interpretation of these regulations or of any to be hereafter issued shall rest entirely with the Royal Aero Club.

3. The competitor shall be solely responsible to the officials for the due observance of these regulations, and shall be the person with whom the officials will deal in respect thereof, or of any other question arising out of this competition.

Q The *Daily Mail* had first offered this prize in 1913. Explain the significance of the first paragraph above. To what does it refer?

Two aviators, John Alcock and Arthur Brown, took up the challenge. They took off from Newfoundland on 14 June 1919 and landed at Clifden, Connemara, on 15 June 1919. It took them 16 hours and 27 minutes.

It was a difficult flight and they nearly didn't make it. They encountered fog, and ice built up on the engines. Brown had to climb out onto the wings during the flight to clear the ice. The cockpit was open, unlike later aircraft cockpits, and Alcock found himself covered in snow sometimes! When they were trying to land in Connemara, they thought they saw a smooth green field below them. However, they discovered it was a bog and they crash-landed, damaging their aircraft. Neither of them was injured.

This is a photograph of Alcock and Brown's plane after landing in Connemara.

This is a statue of Alcock and Brown at Heathrow Airport in London.

Harry Ferguson

Harry Ferguson was brought up on a farm in Co Down. He was one of eleven children but he didn't like farm work. In 1902, he decided to emigrate to Canada. However, his brother Joe had a business in Belfast where he sold and serviced cars and motorbikes. Joe persuaded Harry not to emigrate and to go to work for him instead.

Harry loved this job and was naturally good at mechanical work. He is most famous for his development of the tractor. This tractor became so useful and widely used that it was nicknamed the 'Little Grey Fergie'.

However, he was also interested in motor racing and flying. He visited air shows and exhibitions in France in 1907 and 1908. Then he came back to Ireland and built his own aeroplane.

TIP

PROJECT

BEFORE YOU START

ACTIVITY

BY THE WAY

SOURCES

WORD BOX

LINK

RESEARCH

Questions

1. When very few people were aviators, how do you think Harry Ferguson learnt to fly?

2. Why did he visit air shows and exhibitions before he built his own aeroplane?

Eventually, in 1909, he made his first flight, from Dundrum to Newcastle. This was the first powered flight in Ireland and was in the same year that Blériot had flown across the English Channel.

Harry Ferguson contributed so much to mechanical developments in agriculture, motor cars and aviation that he has been nick-named 'The Mad Mechanic'. In 1990, the Northern Bank issued a £20 note with his portrait on it.

The Ulster Folk and Transport Museum at Cultra, Co Down has a full-scale replica of Harry Ferguson's aeroplane, an early Ferguson tractor and a Ferguson plough on display.

Activity

The Tourist Board has asked you to write and design a double-sided leaflet on Harry Ferguson. The leaflet is to be suitable for leaving in tourist offices, museums and other tourist sites where visitors from overseas might pick it up.

Before you start, you could find out more about Ferguson if you wish.

Plan your leaflet, keeping in mind that you are writing and illustrating it for people who have come from abroad and may not know much about this country.

What would they need to know?

How would the information be best presented?

Would your leaflet be suitable for visitors who don't speak English very well? How could you cater for them?

When you are happy with your plan, word-process your leaflet.

Project

Since the early days of aviation, aircraft have become bigger and more complicated. One of the most remarkable civil aircraft was **Concorde**. In groups, plan a wall display about this aircraft. Everyone in the group must contribute something to the display. One part of your display must contain a list of your sources. Title this "Where We Found our Information". Try to have as many sources as you can and don't just depend on the Internet! You might be able to talk to someone who remembers it. There are also books on Concorde or books that may have a chapter on it.

Review your work

When you have finished your task, have a discussion about it in your group.

Do you think your group worked well together? Why or why not?

Were you pleased with your finished work?

What *two* things did you do really well?

What do you think you could have done better?

Now each person should complete this sentence: "By doing this task, I have learned …"

Your Timeline
Draw a timeline and mark on it all the dates that you have read about in this chapter and what happened on those dates.

Class Quiz!

Divide into two teams and decide on a prize for the winning team. If you get a question right, your team gets a point, BUT if you get a question wrong, you lose a point!

1. Who first crossed the Atlantic by air?

2. "There were no railways in Ireland in 1900." True or false?

3. What newspaper offered prizes for achievements in aviation?

4. In 1903, the speed limit for motor cars was raised from 12 miles per hour. What was it raised to?

5. What is a cow catcher?

6. What is a Zeppelin?

7. Why is the *Hindenburg* famous?

8. Who invented the pneumatic tyre?

9. What was a trolley bus?

10. Apart from London, what city in the UK had the largest fleet of trolley buses?

11. Who was Herbert Morrison?

12. Louis Blériot won a prize for doing what?

13. What motor car manufacturing company opened in Northern Ireland in 1975?

14.   What powers a steam locomotive?

15.   What was the *Flying Scotsman?*

16.   What was a Villa Ticket?

17.   Who wrote the comic song "Are Ye Right There, Michael?"

18.   What sort of trams replaced horse trams in Belfast in 1905?

19.   Why do buses in Londonderry have to have very strong engines?

20.   In the early years of the twentieth century, what mode of transport enabled people to live further away from their work?

Word Check

Check out these words to make sure you can spell them.

commuter	**population**	**Portadown**
electricity	**freight**	**Strabane**
labour	**significant**	**photograph**
Portrush	**locomotive**	**parallel**
carriage	**prairie**	**ordinary**
Leitrim	**diesel**	**peninsula**
community	**Enniskillen**	

If you're not sure if you can spell any of them, check them out a few more times.

FIRST WORLD WAR

BEFORE YOU START

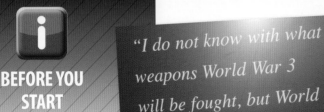

> "I do not know with what weapons World War 3 will be fought, but World War 4 will be fought with sticks and stones."
>
> Albert Einstein

There were many wars in the twentieth century. Some were small and some were very big indeed. Two of the wars were so big and involved so many countries that they are called World Wars. The plaque on the left shows something that Albert Einstein said.

Discuss what you think Einstein meant.

BY THE WAY

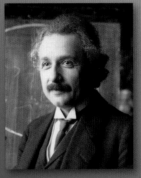

Albert Einstein (1875–1955) is one of the most famous scientists of all time. In 1921, he was awarded the Nobel Prize for Physics. He discovered and wrote about many topics to do with Physics, but he is best known for his Theory of Relativity. He was very intelligent and, although IQ tests had not been invented at the time, it is thought that his IQ score was about 180 (100–120 is about average). After he died his brain was weighed and found to be about 140 grams lighter than that of most people.

Because he was so brainy, his name is often used in a humorous way, eg "Well done, Einstein!"

If you have time, and especially if you like Physics, you could find out more about Einstein.

The First World War, 1914–1918

The First World War is sometimes referred to as 'World War 1'. We call it that because *we* know that there have been *two* world wars. At the time and for years afterwards, it was called The Great War. But how did it begin? Here are two maps which show the political profile of Europe just before the war (Map A) and how it had changed as a result of the war (Map B).

MAP A – Europe 1914

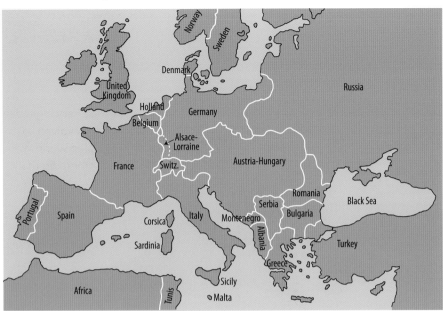

MAP B – Europe 1919

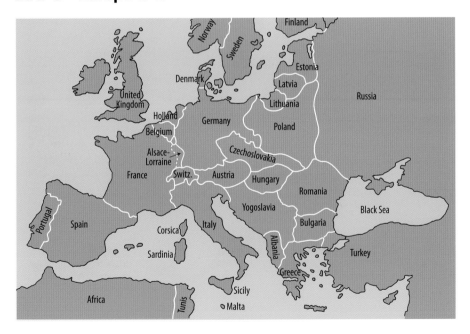

Activity

Talk about these two maps.
What differences do you see?
Where has most of the change occurred?

In 1914, Europe was dominated by a small number of great powers. These countries had divided control in Europe between themselves and had also established colonies all round the world. The amount of land that a country controlled overseas was called an Empire. In 1914, the British Empire was by far the largest.

The Great Powers were:

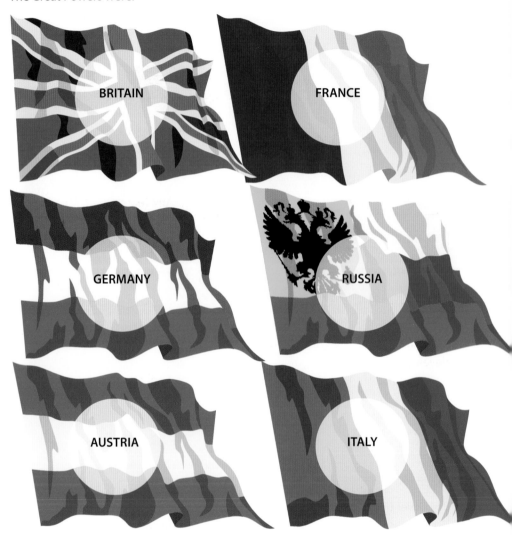

Can you find these countries on the map?

These six countries were constantly trying to improve their own position. This caused anger amongst the others.
For example:

- Germany wanted to build up her navy to match Britain's.

- Germany was increasing her military and industrial strength. This alarmed France and Russia.

- France had lost territory to Germany in 1870 and wanted revenge.

- Austria and Russia wanted to increase their control in South-East Europe. This area was known as **The Balkans**.
- Italy wanted to expand into North Africa but France had occupied Tunisia and annoyed the Italians.

Because of all this, the countries in Europe divided into two power blocs.

TRIPLE ALLIANCE	TRIPLE ENTENTE
GERMANY wanted an Empire	FRANCE wanted revenge
AUSTRIA wanted the Balkans	BRITAIN feared the new German navy
ITALY wanted Tunisia	RUSSIA wanted the Balkans

The countries of the **Triple Alliance** agreed to fight to help each other if a conflict developed.
The countries of the **Triple Entente** had only agreed not to fight against each other if a war developed.
So only one incident involving one country from each of the opposing power blocs was needed to start a major war in Europe.

Activity

Read over this chapter again.
Do you understand why there was so much tension between the countries of Europe in 1914?
If you don't, say which aspects are unclear and have a class discussion about them.

Class discussion

"The countries of Europe are like gangs of bullies in a playground. They should learn some manners and behave like mature, civilised men."

Is this a fair comment on the state of Europe in 1914?

The most likely area for trouble to break out was South-East Europe – The Balkans. There had been small wars here already since 1900. Particularly important was the country of Bosnia, which had been taken over (annexed) by Austria-Hungary. On 28 June 1914, the heir to the Austrian throne, Archduke Franz Ferdinand and his wife Sophie, visited Sarajevo, the capital of Bosnia.

The Archduke and his wife drove through the town, waving to the crowds from their open car, on their way to an official banquet.

This is a photograph of the Archduke and his wife arriving at the banquet.

On the way, there was one attempt to assassinate the Archduke. A grenade was thrown at the car. It missed but injured several people in the car behind.

Because there had been this attack, plans were made to drive the Archduke and his wife back by another route. However, the driver wasn't told of the revised arrangements and took a wrong turn. He was told of his error and backed the car up to change course. Unfortunately, the car paused five feet from another assassin, Gavril Princip, who took his chance and fired two shots at the couple. The first shot hit the Archduke in the throat and the second shot hit his wife in the stomach. They died within minutes.

ASSASSINATION: unlawful killing

This is the car in which they were travelling. It is a 1911 Gräf & Stift open car and is preserved in the Military History Museum, Vienna, Austria.

The assassination had been planned and carried out by Serbian nationalists. Austria-Hungary asked Serbia to hand over the assassins to them but Serbia refused. Nobody expected that events after this would get so bad that they would lead to a great war. It looked as if Austria-Hungary would have a brief war with the much smaller Serbia and then it would all be over.

But look what happened…

SEQUENCE OF EVENTS LEADING TO THE FIRST WORLD WAR

Austria-Hungary declared war on Serbia on 28 July 1914.

- Russia had a treaty with Serbia so it began to get its army ready to attack Austria-Hungary.

- Germany had a treaty with Austria-Hungary and thought that the Russians were about to go to war with Austria-Hungary so Germany declared war on Russia on 1 August 1914.

- France had a treaty with Russia and began to mobilise its armed forces so Germany declared war on France also and because Germany was supporting Austria-Hungary, France was at war with it too.

- Belgium was a neutral country and refused to allow the German army to cross its territory. On 4 August Germany invaded it in order to go the short way to Paris, the capital of France. Britain had a treaty with Belgium to defend it if it was attacked. Britain also had an understanding with France that meant it had a moral obligation to defend France.

- So Britain declared war against Germany on the day it invaded Belgium, 4 August 1914. So now, because of the chain of countries which were at war, Britain was also at war with Austria-Hungary.

- Japan had a military agreement with Britain so it declared war on Germany on 23 August 1914. Two days later Austria-Hungary declared war on Japan.

Questions

The invasion of Belgium by Germany in August 1914 was a very important reason why Britain entered the war. In Britain, there was great support and sympathy for Belgium. This is a cartoon that appeared in *Punch* magazine in August 1914. 'No Thoroughfare' means 'No way through'.

BRAVO, BELGIUM!

1. What do you think the cartoonist is saying in this drawing?

2. Who do the two people represent? How can you tell?

3. What does the gate represent?

4. Whose side do you think the cartoonist is on? Give reasons for your opinion.

5. Why do you think the British were so pleased that Belgium wouldn't allow the Germans to cross their country?

6. What effect do you think this cartoon would have had on those who saw it?

Britain had an Empire at this time and so other countries in the British Empire were affected too and sent soldiers to fight, including Australia, Canada, India, New Zealand and the Union of South Africa.

TIP

PROJECT

BEFORE YOU START

ACTIVITY

BY THE WAY

SOURCES

WORD BOX

LINK

RESEARCH

The United States

In 1914, the President of the United States, Woodrow Wilson, declared that the USA would be neutral in this war. However, in 1917 Germany announced that they were going to use their submarines to attack any ships they came across. Because this was a real threat to America's commercial ships, they decided to enter the war on 6 April 1917.

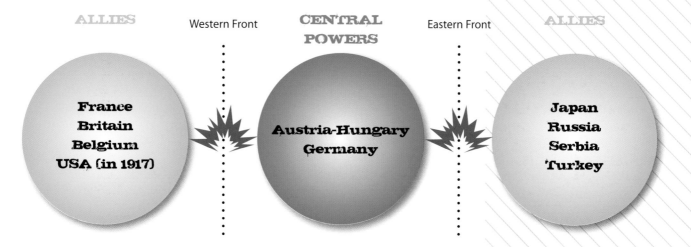

Activity

Countries were drawn into the First World War because they had alliances and treaties with each other. In groups, discuss the advantages and disadvantages of countries having treaties with each other.

One person in each group should be the 'writer' and note down all the points discussed. When you have thought of as much as you can, try to put the advantages in order of importance. Do the same with the disadvantages.

Each group should report back to the class on their discussion. Are the conclusions of the groups all the same or are there differences?

Activity

If you have a best friend, should you support them even if you think they are wrong, or have done something wrong?

If so, how do you justify your support for them?

If not, what could you do instead?

Would you feel the same way if it were someone in your own family?

Project

Here are the names of some of the people who were involved in the war. Choose **one** of them.

Herbert Asquith, Prime Minister (UK)

Lord Kitchener, Minister of War (UK)

David Lloyd George, Prime Minister (UK)

Woodrow Wilson, President (US)

Archduke Friedrich, Commander-in-Chief (Austria-Hungary)

Mustafa Kemal Pasha, General (Turkey)

TE Lawrence, 'Lawrence of Arabia' (UK)

Flora Sandes, Nurse/Serbian Soldier (UK)

You must write a brief article for your local newspaper, explaining who this person is, their background and what part they played in the war. Study some newspaper articles to see how they are laid out.

You will need to start your article with a 'hook'. This is an interesting few sentences that will make the reader want to read on.

Word process your article carefully. Provide sub-headings. Add an illustration if you can.

Review your work

Did you find the person you chose interesting, or did you wish you had picked someone else?

What was the most interesting thing you discovered?

Is there anything more you would like to know about them?

Where did you get your information?

What two things are you pleased about in your work on this project?

What one thing do you think you could have done better?

Because it was thought that the war wouldn't last long and would be an easy victory, young men enlisted in the army very enthusiastically. Their wives and families cheered them as they marched off to war.

Many thought that it would be a big adventure and make a change from life at home.

Many men were unemployed and this was chance to earn a wage.

It was also a way of showing how brave and patriotic you were.

Men from both Britain and Ireland enlisted and in second Ireland Unit we look at the Irish men who volunteered.

36th Irish Brigade march past Belfast City Hall on their way to the Somme, 8th May 1915. Very few of these men survived to return. You will read more about this later in this Unit.

The First World War was one of the largest wars in the whole of history. It is impossible to know how many people died, but estimates vary between 15 million and 20 million. There are about 1.7 million people living in Northern Ireland today.

As the war continued and it became clear that it was going to last years instead of months, fewer wanted to join up. Many posters were put up, encouraging more men to join the army.

Activity

Look at this poster. Lord Kitchener was the British Minister for War.

How is he trying to make people who see it feel? Describe anything about the poster that makes you think this.

Do you think the poster is successful in what it is trying to do?

Why do you think the words 'Another call' have been included? Do they add to the impact of the poster's message?

163

Psychological pressure was put on both men and women.
Look at these two sources.

TO THE WOMEN OF BRITAIN

1. You have read what the Germans have done in Belgium. Have you thought what they would do if they invaded this Country?
2. Do you realise that the safety of your home and children depends on our getting more men NOW.
3. Do you realise that the one word "GO" from you may send another man to fight for our King and Country?
4. When the war is over and someone asks your husband or your son what he did in the Great War, is he to hang his head because you would not let him go?

WONT YOU HELP AND SEND A MAN TO JOIN THE ARMY TODAY?

What effect do you think posters and advertisements like this had on men and women?

Was it fair to target women in order to get men to sign up?

Do you think psychological tactics like these would be effective today?

Conscription and Conscientious Objectors

PSYCHOLOGICAL: to do with the mind.

CONSCRIPTION: a law meaning men (usually) in a certain age group have to join the army. They have no choice.

By 1916, the government in Britain was so short of men for the army that they introduced **conscription**.

But what did you do if you thought it was wrong to fight? There were men who did not believe in violence. There were others who thought *this* war was wrong and refused to take part in it.
These men were called **conscientious objectors**. Often they were treated very badly, beaten up and even imprisoned. They had to go before a military tribunal to explain their views.

Q Usually there was an army officer on the panel of men who interviewed the conscientious objectors. How would this have affected the outcome?

CALLED UP: ordered to join the army.

KHAKI: the colour of the army uniform. Pronounced 'carky'.

By 1915 and 1916, it was clear that there were huge casualties in the war. Men were dying in their thousands. Some women thought that it was very cowardly for men not to join up. They introduced a custom of giving a white feather to any man whom they felt was a coward.

Activity

Read this extract from an article by Francis Beckett in *The Guardian* newspaper on 11 November 2008. He is writing about his grandfather. (At first only unmarried men were called up.)

> "He had three small daughters, which saved him from conscription, and his attempt to volunteer was turned down in 1914 because he was short-sighted. But in 1916, as he walked home to south London from his office, a woman gave him a white feather (an emblem of cowardice). He enlisted the next day. By that time, they cared nothing for short sight. They just wanted a body to stop a shell, which [my grandfather] duly did in February 1918, dying of his wounds on March 28.
>
> My mother was nine, and never got over it. In her last years … she could still talk of his last leave, when he was so shell shocked he could hardly speak and my grandmother ironed his uniform every day in the vain hope of killing the lice.
>
> … Most of all, she blamed that unknown woman who gave him a white feather, and the thousands of brittle, self-righteous women all over the country who had done the same."

The following appeared in the personal column of *The Times* newspaper on July 8 1915:

> "Jack FG. If you are not in khaki by the 20th I shall cut you dead. Ethel M."

1. Do you understand why some women accused men of cowardice if they didn't join up?

2. Do you think that what these women did was right?

3. Explain what the writer means by:

    (i) "They just wanted a body to stop a shell".
    (ii) "brittle, self-righteous women".

4. What does 'Ethel M' mean in her entry in *The Times* personal column?

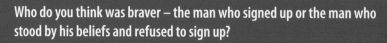

Q Who do you think was braver – the man who signed up or the man who stood by his beliefs and refused to sign up?

If someone feels it is wrong to fight, are there other ways in which he or she can help?

The Trenches

Much of the war on the Western Front (where the British and French faced the Germans) was fought in trenches. These were just what the name says – trenches dug deep into the ground in long, long lines. Both sides dug them and faced each other across the space between. This space became known as 'No Man's Land'.

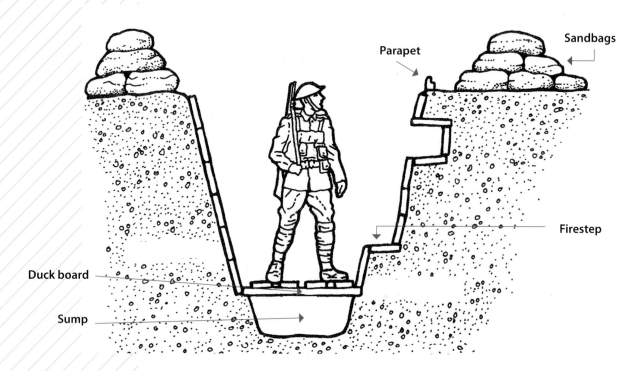

This is a cross-section of a trench. This is what it would have looked like when it was just dug out. During fierce fighting they disintegrated, were blown up, or were flooded and men were wallowing in mud.

Compare this drawing with the photograph of a real trench on the next page. This picture is of a British trench and was taken near the Somme in 1916.

1. Do you see any resemblance between the drawing of the trench and the photograph of a real one?

2. Photographs and film of world events were much less easy to take a hundred years ago. Do you think men would have been so keen to join up if there had been television in 1916, and reports were being shown on the news every day?

3. Is it easier to support a war if you can't see it?

You will find a virtual tour of a trench on this BBC web site: www.bbc.co.uk/history/worldwars/wwone/launch_vt_trench_life.shtml

The soldiers lived in the trenches all the time, except when they had to go into battle. There were some shelters dug into the side of the trenches and areas where some first aid kit was kept.

They were horrible places. If the weather was bad the sides could fall in and the trench would get flooded. Often there were the bodies of dead men lying in the mud for days because no-one could safely leave the trench to bury them.

The two sides in the battles would use rifles to snipe at each other. If a man raised his head above the level of the top of the trench, even for a moment, he was very likely to be shot dead.

As well as the ever-present danger of being shot dead or killed by shrapnel from shells, there were other things that could kill the men. With feet in mud and water all the time, trench foot was common. Here is what one soldier described:

> "If you have never had trench foot described to you, I will explain. Your feet swell to two to three times their normal size and go completely dead. You can stick a bayonet into them and not feel a thing."
>
> *Harry Roberts*

Lice were everywhere:

> "We slept in our clothes and cut our hair short so that it would tuck inside our caps. Dressing simply meant putting on our boots. There were times when we had to scrape the lice off with the blunt edge of a knife and our underclothes stuck to us." *Elizabeth de T'Serclaes – a nurse on the front line.*

Rats infested the trenches and spread disease. Soldiers told of trying to sleep and feeling the rats running over their bodies.

Poisonous gas was used against the enemy. This gas could burn the men's skin and even blind them. Many died from the effects of poison gas.

SNIPE: fire shots from a hidden position when the opportunity arises.

SHRAPNEL: sharp bits of metal from an exploding device.

Communication

Getting messages to and from the trenches to command posts and headquarters was very difficult. Orders had to be sent and reports sent back. Remember how long ago this was – about 100 years ago.

Runners were used to carry messages. A man would be sent from headquarters to run through the trenches giving out the message as he went. If a message had to be taken where there was no trench, the soldier would crawl the whole way there and back again. He was in danger of death all the way.

Telephones were only just beginning to be used. As the war went on, military 'field telephones' were developed. They were very big and heavy and depended on wires being laid between the trenches.

Dogs and pigeons were also used. In fact, pigeons were a most reliable way of sending messages. A piece of paper was rolled up and tied to the pigeon's leg. They were shot at and some of them were injured but still managed to fly on.

They were so important that they had official protection! Read this notice:

SHOOTING HOMING PIGEONS

Killing, wounding or molesting homing pigeons is punishable under the Defence of the Realm Regulations by

SIX MONTHS IMPRISONMENT OR £100 FINE

The public are reminded that homing pigeons are doing valuable work for the government, and are requested to assist in the suppression of the shooting of these birds.

£5 REWARD

will be paid by the National Homing Union for information leading to the conviction of any person SHOOTING HOMING PIGEONS the property of its members.

Activity

Design your own poster about the importance of protecting homing pigeons. Make it more like a poster you would see today. For example, posters today are usually illustrated and use fewer words. Can you think of a catchy line for your poster? Here's one: "Don't take a pop at a pigeon!"

Dogs were able to run across all sorts of terrain with messages tied to their collars. Even so, they faced great dangers.

TERRAIN: an area of land, specially when referring to what its surface is like.

Cher Ami

In October 1918, an American battalion of over 500 men was trapped on a hillside during the Battle of the Argonne in northern France. They were surrounded and under attack by the Germans. Fire from allied troops was also beginning to hit them because the allies didn't know they were there.

Their situation was desperate and the commander sent out a pigeon with a message about their location. This pigeon was shot down. A second pigeon was sent out with another message but this bird was also shot down. By now only 200 men remained alive and many were wounded. There was only one pigeon left – Cher Ami. The commander wrote this note:

The paper was rolled and put in a little canister attached to Cher Ami's leg. The bird was thrown into the air and began to fly. The Germans saw him rising up and bullets flew all round him. He was hit and fell to the ground.

He didn't stay there. Despite being wounded, Cher Ami struggled into the air again and managed to make it to the battalion headquarters, 25 miles away, in less than half an hour. When Cher Ami was found, he had been shot through the breast, blinded in one eye, had one leg almost severed and was covered in blood. But the message had got through and the lives of 194 men were saved.

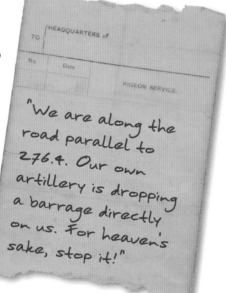

"We are along the road parallel to 276.4. Our own artillery is dropping a barrage directly on us. For heaven's sake, stop it!"

Army doctors worked hard to save the pigeon's life but they couldn't save his leg, so they carved a little wooden leg for him. When he was well enough he was sent back to the United States on a ship. He was treated as a hero and awarded a medal for supreme bravery in the face of danger.

He died in June 1919 and his body is preserved in the National Museum of American History.

'Cher Ami' is French for 'Dear Friend'. Cher Ami was a male pigeon. How would his name be spelt if he were a female pigeon?

Activity

Draw or paint a picture of Cher Ami being tossed into the air with his message. Consider carefully what you will include in your picture. Think about what was going on all around.

This is Cher Ami when he was safely back in the United States, minus a leg and looking a bit worse for wear.

Try this at home

Make a tin can telephone
You will need:

• two empty, clean baked bean tins (or tins like them). Watch out for sharp edges!
• a piece of smooth string. It could be about 3 metres long, but it doesn't have to be an exact length
• something to punch a small hole in the base of the tins

From the outside of the tin, punch a small hole in the middle of the base. It should be just big enough to let the string through and no wider.

Again from the outside, thread one end of the string through the hole into the tin. Tie a knot in the end so that it won't slip out again.

Do the same with the other end of the string and the other tin.

Now hold one tin and get someone else to take the other tin and walk away from you until the string is taut. The string must be taut and you must be in a straight line.

Ask the other person to speak quietly into the tin while you hold the open end of your tin to your ear.

Can you hear them?

If it works well, the sound waves travel along the string and are amplified inside the tin.

Does it work round corners?

AMPLIFIED: made louder.

Activity

This is a very famous picture which hangs in Belfast City Hall. It was painted by JR Beadle. It shows the men of the 36th Ulster Division charging into battle from their trenches at the Battle of the Somme.

- What do you think of the way the battle is portrayed in this picture?
- What is the artist trying to make the viewers feel?
- Describe all the items that the soldiers are carrying.
- Do you think the trenches looked like this at the time?

. . . .

A war is made up of battles. One of the biggest was the Battle of the Somme, which started on 1 July 1916. The Somme is a river in Picardy in northern France. One of the reasons this battle is so famous is because on the very first day, over 20,000 British troops were killed or injured, many of them Ulstermen. There has not been a bigger loss of life in one day in any war since.

Activity

Find the Somme on a map of France.

. . . .

Research

Was the Battle of the Somme worthwhile?
To come to your conclusion, you must investigate what the battle was meant to achieve, what it did achieve and at what cost.

In Northern Ireland this battle is remembered particularly because 5000 men from the 36th Ulster Division were injured. Over 2000 of these men died. The 36th Ulster Division was made up of men who had joined the UVF during the Home Rule Crisis in Ireland. They were preparing to fight to keep Ulster from being included in a new Irish Free State. Their leaders were Sir Edward Carson and Sir James Craig. They told the men in the UVF to enlist in the British Army for two reasons. Firstly, they should support Britain anyway, and secondly, they thought that if they helped Britain in the war, it would make it harder for Britain to force Home Rule on them.

LINK TO SECOND IRELAND UNIT

Nationalists in Ireland also joined the war to fight for Britain. They joined the 10th and 16th Divisions. John Redmond was the leader of the Home Rule Party and he felt that Ireland should support Britain because it would make it harder for Britain to deny them Home Rule when the war was over. Also, Belgium was a small, Catholic country just like Ireland and Redmond felt that Ireland should support all small countries like this.

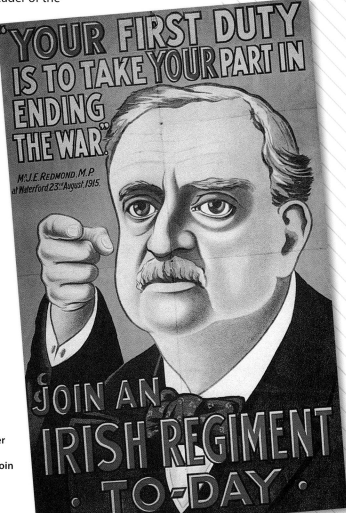

This is a recruitment poster showing John Redmond encouraging Irishmen to join the British Army.
Not all Irish nationalists agreed with Redmond.

Gallipoli

The first big action which the 10th Irish Division saw in the war was at Gallipoli, in the eastern Mediterranean. It joined the Anzac (Australian and New Zealand National Corps) forces and in August 1915 the Irish Division landed on the beaches at Gallipoli, where they were immediately attacked by the Turkish Army. Conditions were dreadful. There wasn't enough water, the heat was terrible and the Turks were very tough enemies.

The battle was fought because the Allies wanted to capture the Turkish city of Constantinople so that they would have a sea route to Russia. From the start it was clear that it had been badly planned and was going to fail. Although they fought very bravely, the 10th Irish Division faced an impossible task and in just over a week 2,000 of its men were killed. In the end, the remains of the Irish Division and all the other parts of the British Army there had to leave.

Activity

Study this photograph. It shows 10th Irish Division troops in a trench at Gallipoli. Describe what you see. What are the conditions like?

The soldiers in the foreground are sleeping.

The helmet that the soldier has on the end of his rifle was of a kind used in the middle-east. What is special about its shape and why is it shaped like this?

Why do you think the soldier is holding up his helmet like this?

Messines

Later in 1917, the 16th Division and the 36th Ulster Division fought side by side at the Battle of Messines, which was in Belgium, close to the French border. This time the Irish soldiers were successful. In June 1917, the 16th and 36th Divisions broke through German lines to score an important victory. The Irish Volunteers and the Ulster Volunteers – Irishmen who had opposed each other at home – joined together to celebrate their victory. At the Battle of Messines the 16th Division had 748 killed and wounded and the 36th had 700 killed and wounded.

The 16th Division lost one of its best known officers. Major Willie Redmond, a Home Rule MP and John Redmond's brother, was killed at Messines.

Write a biography

'The Red Baron' was the nickname of Manfred Albrecht von Richthofen. He was a famous German fighter pilot in the First World War.
Find out more and write a short biography of him.

The Allies won the war by gradually overcoming the other forces. When the United States entered the war in 1917, there were many more men to fight and this made the Allies stronger.

The Armistice (which said that no more shots were to be fired by either side) between the Allies and Germany was signed in a railway carriage in Compiègne Forest on 11 November 1918, and marked the end of the First World War on the Western Front. It was signed at 11.00 am and this is why you may hear that the war ended on the eleventh hour of the eleventh day of the eleventh month.

On the Eastern Front, fighting went on for a while longer.

The **Treaty of Versailles** was signed in 1919. This set out the terms of agreement that all the countries involved had to abide by.

You will have seen people wearing poppies on Remembrance Sunday. This is the second Sunday in November, which is the closest Sunday to the 11 November.

Foot soldiers fought in horrible conditions, in muddy fields and trenches. The poppy was one of the flowers that grew in the fields after the battles. It came to be a symbol for remembrance because it was growing over the buried bodies of so many of the young men who had died.

Activity

There is a famous poem written by a surgeon called John McCrae, who treated men on the battlefield. Flanders is a region which is now in Belgium, France and The Netherlands. Hundreds of thousands of men were killed there, specially at three battles at the town of Ypres.

Read it carefully and answer the questions that follow.

In Flanders Fields

In Flanders fields the poppies blow
Between the crosses, row on row,
That mark our place: and in the sky
The larks, still bravely singing, fly
Scarce heard amid the guns below.

We are the Dead. Short days ago
We lived, felt dawn, saw sunset glow,
Loved, and were loved, and now we lie
In Flanders fields.

Take up our quarrel with the foe:
To you from failing hands we throw
The torch; be yours to hold it high.
If ye break faith with us who die
We shall not sleep,
Though poppies grow
In Flanders fields.

1 How did you feel when you read this poem?

2 Did you want to read it again?

3 From whose point of view is the poem written? Quote from the poem to explain what you think.

4 What do the speakers want the listeners to do?

5 Do you think this poem is in favour of war?

Activity

The British Legion organises the Poppy Appeal every year, coming up to Remembrance Day.

Find out about the British Legion. Their web site is www.britishlegion.org.uk. What do they do?

The Christmas Truce

When the war had been going on for only five months, at Christmas 1914, there was an event which is remembered today as the Christmas Truce. This is what one soldier reported in a letter:

"It was a memorable Christmas Day in our trenches as we had a truce with the enemy from Christmas Eve till Boxing Day morning, not a shot being fired. The truce came about in this way. The Germans started singing and lighting candles about 7.30 on Christmas Eve, and one of them challenged any one of us to go across for a bottle of wine. One of our fellows accepted the challenge; that started the ball rolling. We then went half way to shake hands and exchange greetings with them. There were 10 dead Germans in a ditch in front of the trenches and we helped to bury these. I could have had a helmet but I did not fancy taking one off a corpse. These men were trapped one night while trying to get to our outpost trench some time ago. The Germans seemed to be very nice chaps and said they were awfully sick of the war. We were out of the trenches all Christmas Day collecting souvenirs."

Activity

How do you think the soldier who wrote the letter about the Christmas Truce felt about it?

Compare this account with the poem you read, 'In Flanders Fields'. Is the mood different? Do you think the same person could have written both the poem and the letter?

Why do you think the writer didn't want to take a helmet from a corpse?

The war had to re-start. Here is one Captain's account of what happened at his position on Boxing Day or the day after. He and the German Captain climbed up onto their own parapets:

"We both bowed and saluted and got down again into our respective trenches, and he fired two shots in the air, and the War was on again."

Cpt JC Dunn, Royal Welch Fusiliers

Activity

The British and German soldiers had got to know each other on Christmas Day. In some accounts, they even played games of football together on No-Man's Land. They showed each other pictures of the families they had left at home. Why did they have to fight each other again?
What do you think they felt about this?

Activity

You are a soldier and you have just shot and wounded a German soldier whom you remember chatting to on Christmas Day during the Truce. You know he has a wife and two young children at home. He was very homesick. You don't know if he will die from his wounds.
Write down your feelings in a diary entry.

War Poets

As you have seen in this Unit, war provokes very strong feelings in the people involved. Some of the soldiers in the First World War expressed their feelings through poetry. They have become known as the War Poets.

One of the most famous is Wilfred Owen. He was killed in battle in November 1918, just one week before the war ended. Here is one of his poems (an orison is a prayer):

Anthem for Doomed Youth

What passing bells for these who die as cattle?
Only the monstrous anger of the guns.
Only the stuttering rifles' rapid rattle
Can patter out their hasty orisons.
No mockeries now for them; no prayers nor bells;
Nor any voice of mourning save the choirs,
The shrill, demented choirs of wailing shells;
And bugles calling for them from sad shires.
What candles may be held to speed them all?
Not in the hands of boys, but in their eyes
Shall shine the holy glimmers of good-byes.
The pallor of girls' brows shall be their pall;
Their flowers the tenderness of patient minds,
And each slow dusk a drawing-down of blinds.

How would you describe the mood of this poem? Pick out words from the poem that help you come to your conclusion.

What words would you use to describe how the poet feels?

Do you think this poem helped to make people think more deeply about war?

What does the last line mean?

In line 5, Owen writes "No mockeries now for them". What do you think he is referring to?

Do you think poetry is a good way of expressing feelings?

Research

In pairs, find out about another War Poet. Prepare a presentation for the class explaining a little bit about him and the poetry he wrote. Pick one poem which you really like and read it to the class. If your partner picks a different one, that's all right. Not everyone likes the same things. You could each read your own. Explain what the poet is saying in this poem and why you like it.
Two other War Poets are Rupert Brooke and Siegfried Sassoon.

Project

Your task is to produce a portfolio of information on the sinking of the *Lusitania* on 7 May 1915. To help with your thinking, there are some questions following the Sources and Facts on the following pages.

The *Lusitania* was a passenger ship that sailed on Atlantic crossings between the United States and Europe. It was torpedoed and sunk by a German U-boat (submarine) in 1915.

By the way
'U-boat' is short for the German word for submarine, '*Unterseeboot*'

SOURCES

Source 1

This is an advertisement in a newspaper giving the times of the *Lusitania* sailings to Liverpool. The German Embassy inserted a warning below it.

NOTICE!

Travellers intending to embark on the Atlantic voyage are reminded that a state of war exists between Germany and her allies and Great Britain and her allies; that the zone of war includes the waters adjacent to the British Isles; that, in accordance with formal notice given by the Imperial German Government, vessels flying the flag of Great Britain, or any of her allies, are liable to destruction in those waters and that travellers sailing in the war zone on ships of Great Britain or her allies do so at their own risk.
IMPERIAL GERMAN EMBASSY WASHINGTON, D.C., APRIL 22, 1915.

Source 2

From an article in *The Times* after the sinking:

"…the hideous policy of indiscriminate brutality … has placed the German race outside of the pale. The only way to restore peace in the world, and to shatter the brutal menace, is to carry the war throughout the length and breadth of Germany. Unless Berlin is entered, all the blood which has been shed will have flowed in vain."

Source 3

From the war diary of the captain of the U-boat which fired the torpedo:

"An unusually heavy explosion takes place with a very strong explosion cloud (cloud reaches far beyond front funnel). The explosion of the torpedo must have been followed by a second one (boiler or coal or powder?). The superstructure right above the point of impact and the bridge are torn asunder, fire breaks out, and smoke envelops the high bridge. The ship stops immediately and heels over to starboard very quickly, immersing simultaneously at the bow. It appears as if the ship were going to capsize very shortly. Great confusion ensues on board; the boats are made clear and some of them are lowered to the water with either stem or stern first and founder immediately. On the port side fewer boats are made clear than on the starboard side on account of the ship's list. The ship blows off [steam]; on the bow the name 'Lusitania' becomes visible in golden letters. The funnels were painted black, no flag was set astern. Ship was running twenty knots. Since it seems as if the steamer will keep above water only a short time, we dived to a depth of twenty-four meters and ran out to sea. It would have been impossible for me, anyhow, to fire a second torpedo into this crowd of people struggling to save their lives."

Source 4

A comment from one woman passenger who survived the sinking:

"I don't think we thought of war. It was too beautiful a passage to think of anything like war."

Source 5

Extract from a confidential letter by Winston Churchill, First Lord of the Admiralty, written during the war, but *before* the *Lusitania* was sunk.

"It is most important to attract neutral shipping to our shores, in the hope especially of embroiling the U.S. with Germany. For our part we want the traffic – the more the better and if some of it gets into trouble, better still."

Source 6

Professor William Kingston of Dublin's Trinity College, an expert on British intelligence in World War I, speaking in 2009:

"There's no doubt at all about it that the Royal Navy and the British government have taken very considerable steps over the years to try to prevent whatever can be found out about the *Lusitania*"

Source 7

Reports from *The Times* newspaper, 8 May 1915.

FEARED LOSS OF 1,500 LIVES.

ONLY A FEW FIRST CLASS SAVED.

THE LUSITANIA SUNK.

TORPEDOED OFF IRISH COAST.

NO WARNING.

MANY NOTABLE PASSENGERS.

2,160 ON BOARD.

ONLY 658 KNOWN TO BE SAVED.

The accounts which have so far been received are fragmentary, and give no clear idea of the disaster. There is, however, no doubt that two torpedos were fired without warning into the starboard side of the ship soon after 2 o'clock yesterday afternoon.

Source 8

Gregg Bemis (the owner of the site of the *Lusitania* wreck) believes the British Royal Navy deliberately bombed the *Lusitania* site [in the 1950s] to "make the wreck as unattractive as possible, to prevent further salvage [and to] prevent divers from going in and finding that there was contraband cargo."

Source 9

A poster produced in Ireland after the sinking.

Q

1. Take each SOURCE in turn and write something on each one. Explain what conclusions you can draw from them, if any.
   For example:
   - Can you trust all of the Sources? Why or why not?
   - Which Sources are primary and which are secondary?
   - Are some of the Sources likely to be biased?
   - Add anything else you think of.
2. Look at Source 5. What do you think Churchill meant?
3. Comment on the headlines in Source 7.

FACTS

Fact 1	Although the *Lusitania* was sailing from the USA to Britain, it was a ship of the Cunard Line, a British shipping company.
Fact 2	The USA was neutral at this time.
Fact 3	In 2008, divers discovered millions of rounds of ammunition in the bow section of the ship.
Fact 4	Residents of the town of Cobh, near the site of the wreck, have maintained for years that in the 1950s, the Royal Navy dropped depth charges on the wreck. People on the shore could hear the blasts and saw Royal Navy ships over the area.
Fact 5	The *Titanic*, which had suffered much worse damage when she hit an iceberg in 1912, took over two hours to sink. The *Lustiania* sank in eighteen minutes.
Fact 6	The *Lusitania* was nicknamed 'The Greyhound of the Seas' and was believed to be able to outrun any ship or submarine.
Fact 7	When the *Lusitania* entered Irish waters, the captain was concerned that there were no ships in the area to escort and protect his ship. He had thought there would be.
Fact 8	The *Lusitania* was carrying civilian passengers. About 1153 passengers and crew drowned, many of them children. Of these, 128 were Americans.
Fact 9	A second explosion occurred on board the *Lusitania*, although the U-boat had fired only one torpedo.
Fact 10	The British denied there were any munitions on board and said that the second explosion was caused by coal dust igniting in the ship's hold.
Fact 11	The captain of the U-boat had sunk passenger ships before without warning, although without massive loss of life.

DEPTH CHARGE: a device designed to explode under water.

Q

1. Take each FACT in turn and say how they contribute to the understanding of the sinking. For example:

Fact 5: Was the *Titanic* much bigger than the *Lusitania?* If not, there must be some reason why the *Lusitania* sank so quickly.

Is there anything else you would like to know? If, so, try to find this information.

Plan your portfolio carefully before you start.

You will start with an Introduction. What will your other headings be?

End with an opinion piece, giving your own thoughts and conclusions on the event.

Present your portfolio carefully and neatly, with a contents page and an index.

Review your work

Did you find this a difficult task? Why or why not?

Did you find the subject interesting? You don't have to say 'yes'! If you didn't, explain why you thought it was boring.

What aspect of the task did you enjoy most?

If you had to do this task again, would you do anything differently?

Out of ten, how many marks would you give yourself?

What else would you like to know?

Whole books have been written about the First World War, so it isn't possible to cover everything in this Unit. As you have read and talked about the war, what questions occurred to you?
Make a list of all the queries from the class. Decide how you will find out the answers. As you find the answers, mark off the questions.

Here are some topics you might like to investigate further:

- Developments in aircraft – as well as communication, aviation was one of the things that improved because of the needs of the war.
- War photography – who were the photographers and what did they photograph?
- Rationing – was food rationed during the war?
- What was shell shock?

Class Quiz!

Divide into two teams and decide on a prize for the winning team. If you get a question right, your team gets a point, BUT if you get a question wrong, you lose a point! So think carefully before you answer!

1. What was the real name of The Red Baron?
2. What prize was Albert Einstein awarded in 1921?
3. What were the dates of the First World War?

TIP

PROJECT

BEFORE YOU START

ACTIVITY

BY THE WAY

SOURCES

WORD BOX

LINK

RESEARCH

4. Who was the king of the United Kingdom at the time of the War?

5. What country invaded Belgium in 1914?

6. People were encouraged to shoot pigeons during the war. True or false?

7. Which Irish Division of the army fought at Gallipoli?

8. What does 'Anzac' stand for?

9. Where is the Somme and what happened there in 1916?

10. What did the soldiers use for shelter on the Western Front?

11. What was a man being accused of if he was given a white feather?

12. Some men felt it was wrong to use violence and would not join the army to fight. By what name are they known?

13. Who was the British Minister for War?

14. What is the approximate population of Northern Ireland today?

15. How many people are estimated to have died in the First World War?

16. In what year did the United States enter the war?

17. What does 'U-Boat' stand for?

18. No nationalists from Ireland joined the British Army. True or False?

19. What was nicknamed 'The Greyhound of the Seas'?

20. In what country is Constantinople?

Word Check

Check out these words to make sure you can spell them.

Gallipoli	**advertisement**	**pigeon**
Einstein	**conscription**	**Lusitania**
Belgium	**conscientious**	**torpedo**
Australia	**Guardian**	**recruitment**
biography	**cowardice**	**souvenir**
enthusiastic	**disintegrate**	**Armistice**
psychological	**poisonous**	

If you're not sure if you can spell any of them, check them out a few more times.

CAREERS

So what can I do if I keep on History at school?

As you think about which subjects to study at GCSE, why should you consider keeping on History?

Well, all these people did! ……..

David Sainbsbury (CEO Sainsbury's)
Adam Ant
Jonathan Ross (TV personality)
Sasha Baron Cohen (aka Ali G)
Gordon Brown
Steve Coppell (Crystal Palace manager who played for England in the 1970s)
Diane Abbott (first Afro-Caribbean woman to become an MP)
Gerald Corbett (manager of Manchester United Football Club)
Salman Rushdie (author)
Anita Roddick (Founder of the Body Shop)
Winston Churchill (Prime Minister during the Second World War)
Dermot Murnaghan (TV journalist)
Prince Charles
Jeremy Bowen, BBC correspondent
Penelope Lively, novelist
Elizabeth Chadwick, novelist

David Nicholls, Professor of History at Manchester Metropolitan University comments on the *History Today* website:

"A truly remarkable number [of history graduates] have gone on to become the movers-and-shakers of modern-day Britain. Many top jobs are within the grasp of historians. With a history degree you can aspire to be prime minister, press baron and media mogul, overlord of the BBC, 'the most famous lawyer in the land', Archbishop of Canterbury, top diplomat, Oxbridge vice-chancellor, England footballer or chairman of the richest football club in the world, famous comedian or celebrated pop musician, best-selling novelist, trade union boss, business millionaire …."

www.historytoday.com/MainArticle.aspx?m=18615&amid=18615, accessed 4 August 2009

This all goes to show that that there is an enormous variety of careers open to you if you study history. Let's look at some of the reasons why this is.

Employers in many fields like to see a job applicant who has studied History because it means that the applicant has many skills. With a background in History, you are extremely flexible in which job or career you can target.

Throughout this book you have been asked to put yourself into the position of someone else to try to understand how he or she is feeling about something. There are jobs where your ability to understand other people and to consider their feelings can change you from being good at your job to being great at it. Jobs where this is useful include **receptionist, hairdresser**, **beautician**, **teacher**, **medicine (specially nursing)**, **social work**, **personnel**, **advertising**. Someone who has studied history can consider all these jobs.

Throughout this book you have been asked to find out information, to conduct research. Someone who has studied history has the skills to consider careers as a **TV researcher**, an **investigative reporter**, in **market research**, in **tourism or in the police**.

Throughout this book you have been asked to look at sources and to say if they can be trusted, if they contain bias, what is useful information and what is not. This skill is important for working in **law**, **administration**, **politics, publishing** and **editing**. Many history graduates go into these areas.

Throughout this book you have been asked to write reports, stories, biographies, articles for the media, etc. This would give you an advantage if you wanted to work in the **Civil Service**, **law** or **journalism**. Imagine if you were a reporter reporting on an event and you had no idea of the background to that event! If you have background information in your head, you can be a much better journalist.

Once you have decided in which direction you wish to go, there are many careers which require a post-graduate qualification which allows you to focus more closely on a specialism, for example librarianship, teaching or ICT.

If you want to use history directly in a career, you can consider training as an **archaeologist**, an **archivist**, **museum curator**, a job in **tourism**, an **education officer** in museums and parks, an **antiquarian** or in **art and antique gallery management**.

Of course you could just study History to GCSE level because you like it! That's a good reason. Time travel in your history classes for a while longer and see what you feel in another couple of years.

Whatever you decide to do, remember what poet and philosopher George Santayana said "Those who cannot remember the past are doomed to repeat it."

Best wishes for your future!

> **"I WISH I HAD STUDIED HISTORY AT UNIVERSITY".**
>
> Tony Blair, Prime Minister of the United Kingdom from 2 May 1997 – 27 June 2007

ACKNOWLEDGEMENTS

Colour-Rail: 131

TJ Edgington/Colour-Rail: 130

By kind permission of Belfast City Council: 170

Brian Hilton/Colour-Rail: 133

WE Robertson/Colour-Rail: 41, 140 (upper)

ES Russell/Colour-Rail: 122

Getty Images, Topical Press Agency/Hulton Archive: 45

Haddow Estate: 66

Home Front Heritage Centre: 111

iStockphoto: 5, 20, 24, 30, 36, 38, 50, 114, 118 (top), 119, 146,

Norman Johnston: Coins, 31 (advertisement), 37 (top), 40 (all), 141-143 (all), 173 (lower)

Sheila Johnston, 42, 73 (lower), 117 (top and both lower), 118 (lower)

Dr Wesley Johnston: 35, 96 (upper), 117 (top centre)

Malcolm Johnston: 102 (lower)

RC Ludgate Collection: 129

Mary Evans Picture Library: 49

WT Montgomery: 140 (lower)

Milligan Estate: 91 (top)

National Museum of Ireland: 67, 84, 95, 96 (lower), 97, 99, 100, 101, 102,

Sainsbury Archive, Museum of London Docklands: 12 (both)

Dr Brian S Turner: 103

Tim Webster: 166

Wikipedia Commons: 15, 17, 18, 28, 33 (both), 46 (all), 51, 52 (both), 53, 54, 59, 60, 74, 91 (lower), 118 (top lower), 125, 144, 147 (both), 149, 150 (all), 154, 158 (top), 173 (upper), 176

Linen Hall Library: 75, 80, 82, 83,

Audrey Hodge: 76